Chinese Cooking

Chinese Cooking

H K Lee

Galley Press

Contents

First published in Great Britain in 1983 by
The Octopus Publishing Group
Published in 1988 by Galley Press, an imprint
of W H Smith Limited
Registered No 237811 England
Trading as W H Smith Distributors
St John's House
East Street
Leicester
LE1 6NE
© 1983 Octopus Books Limited
ISBN 0 86136 028 1
Printed in Hong Kong by Mandarin Offset

Introduction

To the Chinese, food is an art form – in the preparation of dishes, great care is taken to provide contrasting flavours, textures both crunchy and soft, and a pleasing variety of colour and shapes (in which vegetables play an important part). As you will see from the many colour photographs in this book, the dishes are as appealing visually as they are satisfying to the appetite. The essence of Chinese cooking is that a very small amount of an expensive food such as meat is used to enhance and 'lift' a much larger amount of fairly bland, relatively inexpensive food such as rice. Economy has always been of paramount concern to the Chinese, but nutritionally their dishes are excellent because, whichever method is used, the ingredients are cooked quickly and therefore retain their natural goodness. It is important, therefore, that the ingredients you buy, especially vegetables, are very fresh and in good condition.

In such a vast country, the repertoire of dishes essentially varies according to regional availability of certain foods, and we can benefit from this enormous variety. Ingredients such as water chestnuts, bamboo shoots and bean sprouts are stocked by the very large supermarkets and specialist delicatessens, while soy sauce and Chinese cabbage are almost as commonplace today as is root ginger – an important flavouring in many Chinese dishes. These specialist Chinese ingredients and seasonings are detailed on page 94.

The basic piece of Chinese cooking equipment is the wok – a large, wide, bowl-shaped pan, which comes with a lid and a special ring base so that it can be placed over gas or electricity. The wok is a very versatile pan, in which you can fry, simmer or steam food. It can be tipped so that the heat reaches the sides, or so that some food can be pushed up away from the hottest area of the pan. An invaluable aid in this method of stir-frying is a kind of fish slice with a flat, scooplike end. Woks and the implements to use with them

NOTES

Standard spoon measurements are used in all recipes;
1 tablespoon=one 15 ml spoon, 1 teaspoon=one 5 ml spoon, all spoon measures are level.

Fresh herbs are used unless otherwise stated. If unobtainable, substitute a bouquet garni of the equivalent herbs, or use dried herbs instead but halve the quantities stated.
Ovens and grills (broilers) should be preheated to specified temperature of heat setting.
For all recipes, quantities are given in metric, imperial and American measures. Follow one set of measures only, because they are not interchangeable.

can be bought from good kitchenware shops and from some Chinese supermarkets. If you have not got a wok, a large, heavy-based frying pan with a lid can be used instead.

Chinese food is often cooked by steaming and this is traditionally done in a bamboo steamer – a set of several tiered bamboo baskets, which allows several kinds of food to be cooked at the same time. Again, these can be bought from some Chinese supermarkets, or you can use an ordinary Western steamer, or even simply place the food to be steamed in a covered heatproof dish over a pan of boiling water.

Apart from these items, Chinese cooking does not require any special equipment, and you can use the implements you already have: whisks, ladles and so on, plus well sharpened knives for all the slicing and chopping that are a vital part of the preparation of any Chinese meal.

When planning a Chinese meal, select foods which complement each other in texture, flavour and colour, ensure that the basic ingredients of each dish are different, and that the dishes are cooked by several different methods – this is because it would be impossible to prepare all the dishes if, for example, they all had to be stir-fried! And bear in mind that all the recipes in this book are designed to be eaten with several other dishes, including plain boiled rice or noodles.

When planning a party, family-style menus are best. For six people you will need five or six main dishes and a soup to be eaten as one of the courses, or in between courses to refresh the palate – rather than as a starter as in the West. It can even be served as the finale to a meal.

Bear in mind that poultry, fish and pork should all be included. If – for example – Peking Roast Duck is your main choice, you could follow this course with various vegetable dishes served with rice, then perhaps a fish course, soup, and sweet and sour. Desserts are not essentially part of a Chinese meal, but if you like to finish a meal in this way there are delicious things to choose from.

When laying the table, knives will not be needed because everything is cut into bite-sized pieces either to cook or to serve it. If you do not have chopsticks, the best aids to eating are forks and spoons. It takes some practice to use chopsticks properly, but it is well worth persevering because they do make for a more authentic meal.

Now to drinks. If you serve a clear broth, this can be the liquid refreshment throughout the meal. Tea is seldom served with the food because most Chinese foods have either been cooked in or contain oil, and tea and oil do not go together but, in China, tea is considered the best after-dinner drink (digestif). Always rinse the teapot thoroughly with boiling water before putting in the tea, use only freshly boiled water and leave the tea to stand for three minutes before serving hot, without milk or sugar, so that the flavour and the fragrance can be enjoyed to the full.

If you prefer to serve wine, of the reds, Burgundy is best with 'big' meat dishes served in a sauce. For stir-fried dishes select a fruity wine (a white Alsace, Orvieto or Frascati from Italy, Pouilly Fumé Blanc from France); if you prefer red, choose a light Italian Valpolicella, Bardolino or Barolo, or a French Beaujolais, Mâcon or Bordeaux.

Eating is a time of pleasure for the Chinese; a time to share and achieve harmony, a time of togetherness. I hope that you will enjoy this experience at *your* table with the recipes from this book.

Soups

BEEF, SPINACH AND TOMATO SOUP

METRIC/IMPERIAL	AMERICAN
225 g/8 oz stewing beef, cut into 12–15 pieces	½ lb beef chuck, cut into 12–15 pieces
2 slices root ginger, peeled and chopped (optional)*	2 slices ginger root, peeled and chopped (optional)*
600 ml/1 pint water	2½ cups water
600 ml/1 pint clear stock	2½ cups clear stock
½ chicken stock cube	1 chicken bouillon cube
4–5 medium tomatoes, quartered	4–5 medium tomatoes, quartered
100–175 g/4–6 oz spinach, chopped	1–1½ cups chopped spinach
2 spring onions, cut into 1 cm/½ inch lengths	2 scallions, cut into ½ inch lengths
salt	salt
freshly ground black pepper	freshly ground black pepper

Place the meat in a large, heavy-bottomed saucepan. Add the ginger and water. Bring to the boil, cover and simmer gently for 1½ hours. Remove the ginger from the pan. Add the stock and crumbled stock (bouillon) cube and return to the boil. Add the tomatoes, spinach and spring onions (scallions). Simmer gently for 3 to 4 minutes. Adjust the seasoning and serve in heated bowls. SERVES 6.

VELVET CRAB CORN SOUP

METRIC/IMPERIAL	AMERICAN
1 litre/1¾ pints chicken stock	4½ cups chicken stock
100–225 g/4–8 oz crab meat, flaked	½–1 cup flaked crab meat
225 g/8 oz sweetcorn, cooked	1½ cups whole kernel corn, cooked
salt	salt
1 tablespoon cornflour	1 tablespoon cornstarch
2 tablespoons water	2 tablespoons water
2 egg whites	2 egg whites
2 tablespoons milk	2 tablespoons milk
¼ teaspoon sesame seed oil*	¼ teaspoon sesame seed oil*
few drops of hot pepper oil or hot pepper sauce	few drops of hot pepper oil or hot pepper sauce

Place the chicken stock in a large pan and bring to the boil, then add the crab meat, sweet corn and salt to taste. Blend the cornflour (cornstarch) with the water and add to the pan. Heat, stirring until the mixture comes to the boil and thickens.

Beat egg whites and milk lightly together. Remove pan from heat and add the egg whites, stirring constantly. Season with sesame oil and hot pepper oil or sauce. Serve immediately in heated bowls. SERVES 6.

SOUP OF THE GODS (EGG-DROP SOUP)

METRIC/IMPERIAL	AMERICAN
1 chicken stock cube	2 chicken bouillon cubes
600 ml/1 pint hot stock	2½ cups hot stock
1 egg, beaten	1 egg, beaten
2–3 spring onions, cut into rings	2–3 scallions, cut into rings
1 teaspoon sesame seed oil*	1 teaspoon sesame seed oil*
salt	salt
freshly ground black pepper	freshly ground black pepper

Dissolve the stock (bouillon) cube in the hot stock in a saucepan. Bring to the boil, remove from the heat and dip the egg in a narrow stream along the prongs of a fork into the stock, trailing it over the surface. Do not stir until the egg has set (not more than 15 seconds).

To serve, divide the spring onions (scallions) between 4 heated individual serving bowls. Pour the soup into the bowls and sprinkle with sesame oil and salt and pepper. SERVES 4.

ABALONE AND GREEN PEA SOUP

METRIC/IMPERIAL	AMERICAN
1.2 litres/2 pints pork stock	5 cups pork stock
100 g/4 oz lean pork, shredded	½ cup shredded lean pork
4 Chinese dried mushrooms, soaked in warm water for 30 minutes*	4 Chinese dried mushrooms, soaked in warm water for 30 minutes*
100 g/4 oz shelled peas	¾ cup shelled peas
1 small can abalone	1 small can abalone
1 tablespoon soy sauce*	1 tablespoon soy sauce*

Pour the stock into a large pan and bring to the boil. Add the pork and simmer for 5 minutes. Drain the mushrooms, squeeze dry, discard stems and slice. Add the peas and mushrooms to the stock and simmer for 10 minutes. Drain the abalone, reserving the juice, and cut into small pieces. Add the abalone to the pan with the juice and soy sauce. Stir and serve immediately in heated bowls. SERVES 6 to 8.

Beef, Spinach and Tomato Soup

DUCK AND CABBAGE SOUP

METRIC/IMPERIAL	AMERICAN
1 duck carcass, with giblets	1 duck carcass, with giblets
2 slices root ginger, peeled*	2 slices ginger root, peeled*
450 g/1 lb Chinese cabbage, sliced	1 lb bok choy, sliced
salt	salt
freshly ground black pepper	freshly ground black pepper

Break up the duck carcass and place in a large saucepan. Add the giblets and any other meat left over from the duck. Cover with water, add the ginger and bring to the boil. Skim, then lower the heat, cover and simmer gently for 30 to 40 minutes.

Add the cabbage (bok choy) and salt and pepper to taste. Continue cooking for another 20 minutes. Remove the duck carcass and ginger with a slotted spoon. Adjust the seasoning and serve hot in heated bowls. SERVES 6 to 8.

SHREDDED PORK AND NOODLES IN SOUP

METRIC/IMPERIAL	AMERICAN
3–4 Chinese dried mushrooms, soaked in warm water for 30 minutes*	3–4 Chinese dried mushrooms, soaked in warm water for 30 minutes*
225 g/8 oz lean pork, shredded	1 cup shredded pork loin
1 tablespoon soy sauce*	1 tablespoon soy sauce*
1 tablespoon medium or dry sherry	1 tablespoon medium or pale dry sherry
1 teaspoon sugar	1 teaspoon sugar
2 teaspoons cornflour	2 teaspoons cornstarch
350 g/12 oz egg noodles	¾ lb egg noodles
salt	salt
3 tablespoons vegetable oil	3 tablespoons vegetable oil
2 spring onions, cut into 2.5 cm/1 inch lengths	2 scallions, cut into 1 inch lengths
100 g/4 oz bamboo shoots, shredded*	1 cup shredded bamboo shoots*
600 ml/1 pint boiling chicken stock	2½ cups boiling chicken stock

Drain the mushrooms, reserving liquid, squeeze dry and remove the stems. Place the pork in a bowl with the soy sauce, sherry, sugar and cornflour (cornstarch). Stir well and leave to marinate for 20 minutes. Cook the noodles in boiling, salted water for about 5 minutes, then drain and keep hot.

Heat 1½ tablespoons oil in a wok or frying pan (skillet), then add the pork and stir-fry until it changes colour. Remove from the pan with a slotted spoon and drain.

Heat the remaining oil in the wok or frying pan (skillet), add the spring onions (scallions), mushrooms and bamboo shoots. Stir, then add a little salt. Return the pork to the pan together with the soaking liquid from the mushrooms.

Place the noodles in a large serving bowl, pour over the boiling stock, then add the pork and vegetables. Serve hot. SERVES 4.

CAULIFLOWER GRUEL

METRIC/IMPERIAL	AMERICAN
1 small cauliflower, finely chopped	1 small cauliflower, finely chopped
100 g/4 oz chicken, coarsely chopped	½ cup coarsely chopped chicken
1 litre/1¾ pints chicken stock	4¼ cups chicken stock
2 eggs, beaten	2 eggs, beaten
1 teaspoon salt	1 teaspoon salt
50 g/2 oz lean ham, finely chopped	¼ cup finely chopped lean ham
chopped coriander leaves, to garnish	chopped coriander leaves, for garnish

Place the cauliflower, chicken and stock in a saucepan and bring to the boil. Cover and cook gently for 15 to 20 minutes. Pour the eggs into the soup then stir in the salt and ham. Pour into a warmed soup tureen and sprinkle with the coriander. Serve hot. SERVES 4.

WATERMELON SOUP

Duck and Cabbage Soup; Shredded Pork and Noodles in Soup; Cauliflower Gruel

METRIC/IMPERIAL	AMERICAN
4–5 Chinese dried mushrooms, soaked in warm water for 30 minutes*	4–5 Chinese dried mushrooms, soaked in warm water for 30 minutes*
1 medium watermelon	1 medium watermelon
600 ml/1 pint stock	2½ cups stock
1 large piece bamboo shoot, sliced*	1 large piece bamboo shoot, sliced*
50 g/2 oz cooked ham, diced	¼ cup diced cooked ham
2 slices root ginger, peeled and shredded*	2 slices ginger root, peeled and shredded*
1 chicken stock cube	2 chicken bouillon cubes
2 teaspoons dried shrimps*	2 teaspoons dried shrimp*
2 tablespoons dry sherry	2 tablespoons dry sherry
½ teaspoon salt	½ teaspoon salt

Drain the mushrooms, squeeze dry, discard stems and cut into quarters. Halve the melon crosswise and scoop out the

flesh and seeds from the lower half. Slice a quarter of the flesh to the same size as the bamboo shoot. Remove the seeds and some of the flesh from the upper half of the melon and use as a lid for the lower half.

Heat the stock in a saucepan, then add all the ingredients, except the melon shells. Bring to the boil, cover and simmer for 30 minutes. Stand the scooped-out melon shell in a heat proof bowl and pour in the soup. Place the other melon shell on top as a lid and put the bowl with the melon in a steamer and steam for 45 minutes.

To serve, remove the bowl from the steamer and ladle out the soup from the melon into heated bowls. SERVES 4.

TOMATO SOUP WITH EGG FLOWER

METRIC/IMPERIAL	AMERICAN
1 tablespoon vegetable oil	*1 tablespoon vegetable oil*
4 tomatoes, peeled and sliced	*4 tomatoes, peeled and sliced*
1 onion, roughly chopped	*1 onion, roughly chopped*
900 ml/1½ pints chicken stock	*3¾ cups chicken stock or broth*
salt	*salt*
freshly ground black pepper	*freshly ground black pepper*
pinch of monosodium glutamate*	*pinch of monosodium glutamate**
1 egg, beaten	*1 egg, beaten*

Heat the oil in a large saucepan. Add the tomatoes and onion and sauté for 5 minutes or until softened but not browned. Pour off any excess oil, then add the stock, salt and pepper and monosodium glutamate. Bring to the boil, cover and simmer for 30 minutes. Add the egg slowly, stirring constantly until it separates into shreds. SERVES 4.

MIXED VEGETABLE SOUP WITH SHREDDED BACON

METRIC/IMPERIAL	AMERICAN
1.25 litres/2¼ pints clear stock	*5½ cups clear stock or broth*
2 rashers streaky bacon, cut into matchstick strips	*2 slices bacon, cut into matchstick strips*
75 g/3 oz French beans, trimmed and halved	*½ cup trimmed and halved green beans*
½ red pepper, cored, seeded and diced	*½ red pepper, cored, seeded and diced*
1 medium onion, thinly sliced	*1 medium onion, finely sliced*
2 celery sticks, cut into 2.5 cm/1 inch lengths	*2 stalks celery, cut into 1 inch lengths*
75 g/3 oz transparent noodles, soaked in warm water for 10 minutes	*3 oz cellophane noodles, soaked in warm water for 10 minutes*
1 chicken stock cube	*2 chicken bouillon cubes*
3 medium tomatoes, cut into wedges	*3 medium tomatoes, cut into wedges*
50 g/2 oz watercress, chopped	*½ cup chopped watercress*
3–4 lettuce leaves, shredded	*3–4 lettuce leaves, shredded*
1½ tablespoons soy sauce*	*1½ tablespoons soy sauce**
2 spring onions, cut into 1 cm/½ inch lengths	*2 scallions, cut into ½ inch lengths*
salt	*salt*
freshly ground black pepper	*freshly ground black pepper*

Pour the stock into a large saucepan. Add the bacon, beans, pepper, onion, celery, noodles and crumbled stock (bouillon) cube(s). Bring to the boil, cover and simmer gently for 15 minutes.

Add the tomatoes, watercress, lettuce, soy sauce, spring onions (scallions) and salt and pepper to taste. Simmer for a further 5 minutes. Serve in heated bowls. SERVES 6.

Shrimp, Chicken and Sweetcorn Soup; Chicken and Mushroom Soup; Mixed Vegetable Soup with Shredded Bacon

CHICKEN AND MUSHROOM SOUP

METRIC/IMPERIAL	AMERICAN
8 medium Chinese dried mushrooms, soaked in warm water for 30 minutes*	8 medium Chinese dried mushrooms, soaked in warm water for 30 minutes*
1 × 1 kg/2–2½ lb chicken	1 (2–2½ lb) broiler/fryer
1 tablespoon medium or dry sherry	1 tablespoon cream or pale dry sherry
1 spring onion	1 scallion
1 slice root ginger, peeled*	1 slice ginger root, peeled*
1½ teaspoons salt	1½ teaspoons salt

Drain the mushrooms, reserving the soaking liquid. Squeeze dry and discard the stems.

Place the chicken in a large pan and cover with boiling water. Boil rapidly for 2 to 3 minutes, then remove the chicken and rinse thoroughly under cold running water.

Place the chicken and mushrooms in a pan or casserole with a tight-fitting lid. Add just enough water to cover the chicken, then add the sherry, spring onion (scallion), ginger and reserved soaking liquid from the mushrooms. Bring to the boil, lower the heat, cover and simmer for 2 to 2½ hours.

Just before serving skim the surface to remove any impurities. Discard the spring onion (scallion) and ginger, if desired. Stir in the salt and pour into a warmed soup tureen. Serve immediately. SERVES 4.

SHRIMP, CHICKEN AND SWEETCORN SOUP

METRIC/IMPERIAL	AMERICAN
1 × 326 g/11½ oz can sweetcorn, drained	1 can (12 oz) whole kernel corn, drained
100–175 g/4–6 oz peeled shrimps	²⁄₃–¾ cup shelled shrimp
100 g/4 oz boned chicken breast, cut into cubes	¼ lb boned chicken breast, cut into cubes
100 g/4 oz shelled peas	¾ cup shelled peas
1 chicken stock cube	2 chicken bouillon cubes
300 ml/½ pint water	1¼ cups water
300 ml/½ pint cold clear stock	1¼ cups cold clear stock
1½ tablespoons cornflour	1½ tablespoons cornstarch
salt	salt
freshly ground black pepper	freshly ground black pepper

Place the sweetcorn in a large pan with the shrimps, chicken, peas, crumbled stock (bouillon) cube(s) and water. Bring to the boil, cover and simmer for 2 to 3 minutes.

Blend the stock with the cornflour (cornstarch) and add to the soup. Heat, stirring until the soup thickens and continue to cook for 1 minute. Add salt and pepper to taste, then pour into heated bowls. SERVES 4.

Fish & Shellfish

CRAB OMELET

METRIC/IMPERIAL	AMERICAN
2 spring onions	2 scallions
4 eggs, beaten	4 eggs, beaten
salt	salt
3 tablespoons vegetable oil	3 tablespoons vegetable oil
2 slices root ginger, peeled and shredded*	2 slices ginger root, peeled and shredded*
175 g/6 oz fresh, frozen or canned crab meat	6 oz fresh, frozen or canned crab meat
1 tablespoon medium or dry sherry	1 tablespoon cream or pale dry sherry
1½ tablespoons soy sauce*	1½ tablespoons soy sauce*
2 teaspoons sugar	2 teaspoons sugar
To garnish:	For garnish:
shredded lettuce	shredded lettuce
tomato and grape (optional)	tomato and grape (optional)

Cut the white part of the spring onion (scallions) into 2.5 cm/1 inch lengths. Chop the green parts finely and beat into the eggs. Add salt to taste.

Heat the oil in a wok or frying pan (skillet). Add the white spring onions (scallions) and the ginger, then the crab and sherry. Stir-fry for a few seconds then add the soy sauce and sugar. Lower the heat, pour in the egg mixture and cook for a further 30 seconds.

Transfer to a serving plate and garnish with shredded lettuce. SERVES 4.

DEEP-FRIED PRAWNS (SHRIMP) IN SHELLS

METRIC/IMPERIAL	AMERICAN
450 g/1 lb raw unpeeled prawns	1 lb raw shrimp, unshelled
2 slices root ginger, peeled and finely chopped*	2 slices ginger root, peeled and finely chopped*
1 teaspoon medium or dry sherry	1 teaspoon cream or dry sherry
1½ teaspoons cornflour	1½ teaspoons cornstarch
450 ml/¾ pint vegetable oil, for deep-frying	2 cups vegetable oil, for deep-frying
1 teaspoon salt	1 teaspoon salt
1 teaspoon chilli sauce (optional)	1 teaspoon chili sauce (optional)
To garnish:	For garnish:
coriander leaves	coriander leaves
lemon peel (optional)	lemon peel (optional)

Place the unpeeled prawns (shrimp) in a bowl with the ginger, sherry and cornflour (cornstarch). Stir gently to mix then leave in the refrigerator to marinate for 20 minutes.

Heat the oil in a wok or deep-fryer to 180°C/350°F. Lower the heat, add the prawns and deep-fry for 1 minute. Remove and drain on kitchen paper towels.

Allow the oil to cool then pour into another container. Return the prawns (shrimp) to the wok or fryer and add the salt and chilli sauce. Mix well and heat through. Serve hot garnished with coriander leaves and lemon peel. SERVES 4.

STIR-FRIED SQUID WITH MIXED VEGETABLES

METRIC/IMPERIAL	AMERICAN
450 g/1 lb squid	1 lb squid
2 slices root ginger, peeled and finely chopped*	2 slices ginger root, peeled and finely chopped*
1 tablespoon dry sherry	1 tablespoon pale dry sherry
1 tablespoon cornflour	1 tablespoon cornstarch
15 g/½ oz wood ears, soaked in warm water for 20 minutes*	½ cup tree ears, soaked in warm water for 20 minutes*
4 tablespoons vegetable oil	¼ cup vegetable oil
2 spring onions, white part only, cut into 2.5 cm/1 inch lengths	2 scallions, white part only, cut into 1 inch lengths
225 g/8 oz broccoli, divided into florets	½ lb broccoli, divided into florets
2 medium carrots, peeled and cut into diamond-shaped chunks	2 medium carrots, peeled and cut into diamond-shaped chunks
1 teaspoon salt	1 teaspoon salt
1 teaspoon sugar	1 teaspoon sugar
1 teaspoon sesame seed oil*	1 teaspoon sesame seed oil*

Clean the squid, discarding the head, transparent backbone and ink bag. Cut the flesh into thin slices or rings. Place in a bowl with half the ginger, the sherry and cornflour (cornstarch). Mix well and leave to marinate for 20 minutes. Drain the wood (tree) ears and break into small pieces, discarding the hard bits.

Heat half of the oil in a wok or frying pan (skillet). Add the spring onions (scallions) and remaining ginger, the broccoli, carrots and wood (tree) ears. Stir-fry for 2 minutes, add the salt and sugar, and continue to cook until the vegetables are tender, adding a little water if necessary. Remove from the pan with a slotted spoon and drain.

Heat the remaining oil in the pan, add the squid and stir-fry for about 1 minute. Return the vegetables to the pan, with the sesame seed oil and mix all the ingredients well together. Spoon onto a hot serving platter and serve immediately. SERVES 4.

Stir-fried Squid with Mixed Vegetables; Crab Omelet

PRAWN (SHRIMP) BALLS WITH BROCCOLI

METRIC/IMPERIAL	AMERICAN
225 g/8 oz unpeeled Dublin Bay prawns	½ lb unshelled jumbo shrimp or Pacific prawns
1 slice root ginger, peeled and finely chopped*	1 slice ginger root, peeled and finely chopped*
1 teaspoon medium or dry sherry	1 teaspoon cream or dry sherry
1 egg white	1 egg white
1 tablespoon cornflour	1 tablespoon cornstarch
3 tablespoons vegetable oil	3 tablespoons vegetable oil
2 spring onions, finely chopped	2 scallions, finely chopped
225 g/8 oz broccoli, cut into small pieces	½ lb broccoli, cut into small pieces
1 teaspoon salt	1 teaspoon salt
1 teaspoon sugar	1 teaspoon sugar

Wash the unshelled prawns (shrimp), dry with kitchen paper towels, then use a sharp knife to make a shallow cut down the back of each prawn and pull out the black intestinal vein. Split each prawn in half lengthwise, then cut into small pieces.

Place the prawns into a bowl with the ginger, sherry, egg white and cornflour (cornstarch). Stir well and leave in the refrigerator to marinate for 20 minutes.

Heat 1 tablespoon oil in a wok or frying pan (skillet), add the prawns and stir-fry over moderate heat until they change colour. Remove from the pan with a slotted spoon.

Heat the remaining oil in the wok or frying pan (skillet), add the spring onions (scallions) and broccoli. Stir, then add the salt and sugar. Heat until the broccoli is just tender, then add the prawns (shrimp) and still well. Spoon onto a hot serving platter and serve immediately. SERVES 4.

BEAN CURD AND PRAWNS (SHRIMP)

METRIC/IMPERIAL	AMERICAN
3 tablespoons vegetable oil	3 tablespoons vegetable oil
6 cakes bean curd, sliced into 5 mm/¼ inch thick slices and each slice cut into 5–6 pieces*	6 cakes bean curd, sliced into 5 mm/¼ inch thick slices and each slice cut into 5–6 pieces*
½ teaspoon salt	½ teaspoon salt
1 teaspoon sugar	1 teaspoon sugar
1 teaspoon medium or dry sherry	1 teaspoon cream or pale dry sherry
2 tablespoons soy sauce*	2 tablespoons soy sauce*
50 g/2 oz peeled prawns	⅓ cup shelled shrimp
shredded spring onions, green part only, to garnish	shredded scallions, green part only, for garnish

Heat the oil in a wok or frying pan (skillet). Add the bean curd and stir-fry until golden on all sides. Add the salt, sugar, sherry and soy sauce and stir-fry for a few seconds. Add the prawns (shrimp), stir gently and cook for 1 to 2 minutes. Serve hot, garnished with shredded spring onion (scallion). SERVES 4.

BRAISED FISH WITH SPRING ONIONS (SCALLIONS) AND GINGER

METRIC/IMPERIAL	AMERICAN
1 × 750 g/1½ lb whole fish	1 × 1½ whole fish
1 teaspoon salt	1 teaspoon salt
2 tablespoons flour	2 tablespoons flour
3 tablespoons vegetable oil	3 tablespoons vegetable oil
3–4 spring onions, cut into 2.5 cm/1 inch lengths	3–4 scallions, cut into 1 inch lengths
2–3 slices root ginger, peeled and shredded*	2–3 slices ginger root, peeled and shredded*
Sauce:	Sauce:
2 tablespoons soy sauce*	2 tablespoons soy sauce*
2 tablespoons medium or dry sherry	2 tablespoons cream or pale dry sherry
150 ml/¼ pint chicken stock or water	⅔ cup chicken broth or water
1 teaspoon cornflour	1 teaspoon cornstarch
freshly ground black pepper	freshly ground black pepper
To garnish:	For garnish:
tomato halves	tomato halves
coriander leaves	coriander leaves
cherries	cherries

Prawn Balls with Broccoli; Braised Fish with Spring Onions and Ginger

KING PRAWNS IN SHELL WITH TOMATO SAUCE

METRIC/IMPERIAL	AMERICAN
1 kg/2 lb raw king prawns, peeled and deveined, but with tail shells intact	2 lb raw jumbo shrimp, shelled and deveined, but with tail shells intact
2 tablespoons oil	2 tablespoons oil
2 tablespoons Chinese wine or sherry	2 tablespoons Chinese wine or sherry
1 teaspoon sesame seed oil*	1 teaspoon sesame seed oil*
Gravy:	Gravy:
1½ tablespoons tomato ketchup	1½ tablespoons tomato ketchup
1 tablespoon chilli sauce	1 tablespoon chili sauce
pinch of salt	pinch of salt
¼ teaspoon sugar	¼ teaspoon sugar
2 tablespoons chicken stock	2 tablespoons chicken stock
½ teaspoon monosodium glutamate*	½ teaspoon monosodium glutamate*
1 tablespoon shredded root ginger*	1 tablespoon shredded ginger*
½ teaspoon cornflour	½ teaspoon cornstarch
2 teaspoons water	2 teaspoons water

If the prawns are very large, cut them in half. Heat a wok or frying pan (skillet), add the oil and stir-fry the prawns until red, about 2 minutes. Sprinkle with Chinese wine or sherry.

Place the gravy ingredients in a bowl and blend together. Stir into the prawns, cover and bring to the boil. Reduce the heat and simmer gently for 3 to 4 minutes. Add the sesame oil and serve immediately. SERVES 6 to 8.

PRAWN BALLS

METRIC/IMPERIAL	AMERICAN
100 g/4 oz self-raising flour	1 cup self-raising flour
salt	salt
1 egg	1 egg
150 ml/¼ pint water	⅔ cup water
2 tablespoons cornflour	2 tablespoons cornstarch
½ teaspoon white pepper	½ teaspoon white pepper
pinch of monosodium glutamate*	pinch of monosodium glutamate*
450 g/1 lb king prawns, peeled and cut into 2.5 cm/1 inch pieces	1 lb jumbo shrimp, shelled and cut into 1 inch pieces
peanut oil for deep frying	peanut oil for deep frying
parsley sprigs, to garnish	parsley sprigs, for garnish

Slash both sides of the fish diagonally with a sharp knife at 5 mm/¼ inch intervals as far as the bone. Rub the fish inside and out with the salt, then coat with the flour.

Heat the oil in a large wok or frying pan (skillet) until very hot. Lower the heat a little, add the fish and fry for about 2 minutes on each side, or until golden and crisp, turning the fish carefully. Remove from the pan.

Place the sauce ingredients in a bowl and blend together.

Add the spring onions (scallions) and ginger to the oil remaining in the wok. Stir-fry for a few seconds then stir in the sauce mixture and return the fish to the pan.

Simmer for a few minutes then carefully transfer the fish to a warmed serving dish. Pour the sauce over the fish and garnish with tomato halves, trimmed with coriander leaves and cherries. Serve immediately. SERVES 4.

Sift the flour into a bowl with a pinch of salt. Make a well in the centre and add the egg. Using a wooden spoon, mix the flour into the egg. Add half the water and continue mixing. Beat thoroughly and stir in the remaining water. Mix the cornflour (cornstarch) with ½ teaspoon salt, the pepper and monosodium glutamate. Coat the prawn (shrimp) pieces in the seasoned cornflour (cornstarch) and dip into the batter.

Heat the peanut oil in a wok or deep-fryer to 180°C/350°F and deep-fry the prawns (shrimp) until crisp and golden. Drain on kitchen paper towels. Arrange the prawns (shrimp) on a hot serving platter and garnish with the parsley. SERVES 6.

ONION AND GINGER CRAB WITH EGG SAUCE

METRIC/IMPERIAL	AMERICAN
2–3 medium crabs	2–3 medium crabs
2 teaspoons salt	2 teaspoons salt
4–5 slices root ginger, peeled and shredded*	4–5 slices ginger root, peeled and shredded*
1 tablespoon soy sauce*	1 tablespoon soy sauce*
1 tablespoon chilli sauce	1 tablespoon chili sauce
2 tablespoons dry sherry	2 tablespoons dry sherry
150 ml/¼ pint clear stock	⅓ cup clear stock
5 tablespoons vegetable oil	⅓ cup vegetable oil
2 medium onions, thinly sliced	2 medium onions, thinly sliced
4 garlic cloves, crushed	4 garlic cloves, crushed
3–4 spring onions, cut into 2.5 cm/1 inch lengths	3–4 scallions, cut into 1 inch lengths
1 egg, beaten	1 egg, beaten

Separate the main shell from the body of each crab by inserting a knife under the shell. Crack the claws and shells and chop each body into quarters. Scrape out and remove all the spongy parts. Rub the crab body all over with salt and ginger. Combine the soy sauce, chilli sauce, sherry and stock until well blended.

Heat the oil in a large frying pan (skillet). Add the onions and garlic, then stir-fry for 30 seconds. Add the crab pieces and stir-fry for 3 to 4 minutes until well cooked through. Add the spring onions (scallions) and stir-fry for another 3 to 4 minutes. Pour the sauce mixture over the crab pieces and stir-fry for a further 1½ minutes. When the sauce begins to froth, add the beaten egg in a thin stream.

To serve, turn the mixture onto a warmed serving dish. SERVES 6 to 8.

QUICK-FRIED PRAWNS (SHRIMP) WITH BACON, MUSHROOMS AND CUCUMBER

METRIC/IMPERIAL	AMERICAN
350–450 g/¾–1 lb peeled prawns	¾–1 lb shelled shrimp
2 garlic cloves, crushed	2 garlic cloves, crushed
2 slices root ginger, peeled and chopped (optional)*	2 slices ginger root, peeled and chopped (optional)*
4 tablespoons vegetable oil	4 tablespoons vegetable oil
1 teaspoon salt	1 teaspoon salt
freshly ground black pepper	freshly ground black pepper
15 g/½ oz butter	1 tablespoon butter
1 medium onion, thinly sliced	1 medium onion, thinly sliced
225–350 g/8–12 oz mushrooms, chopped	2–2½ cups chopped mushrooms
2–3 rashers streaky bacon, cut into thin strips	2–3 slices bacon, cut into thin strips
½ medium cucumber, cut into 1 cm/½ inch cubes	½ medium cucumber, cut into ½ inch cubes
1 teaspoon sugar	1 teaspoon sugar
1½ tablespoons soy sauce*	1½ tablespoons soy sauce*
2 tablespoons dry sherry	2 tablespoons dry sherry
450 g/1 lb hot cooked rice	6 cups hot cooked rice

Rub the prawns (shrimp) all over with the garlic, ginger and 1 tablespoon oil. Sprinkle with salt and pepper.

Heat the remaining oil and the butter in a large frying pan (skillet) over high heat, then add the onion. Stir-fry for 30 seconds. Add the mushrooms and bacon and stir-fry for 1 minute. Add the prawns (shrimp) and cucumber and sprinkle on the sugar and soy sauce. Stir-fry for 2 minutes. Stir in the sherry and cook for a few seconds.

To serve, arrange the cooked rice on a warmed serving platter and spoon the prawn (shrimp) mixture on top. SERVES 6.

STEAMED LOBSTER

METRIC/IMPERIAL	AMERICAN
1 × 1–1½ kg/2–3 lb cooked lobster, cut in half, black matter and spongy parts removed	2–3 lb cooked lobster, cut in half, black matter and spongy parts removed
2 teaspoons salt	2 teaspoons salt
½ teaspoon monosodium glutamate*	½ teaspoon monosodium glutamate*
2 garlic cloves, crushed	2 garlic cloves, crushed
1 tablespoon dry sherry	1 tablespoon dry sherry
1 tablespoon vegetable oil	1 tablespoon vegetable oil
2 onions, thinly sliced	2 onions, thinly sliced
Dip:	Dip:
4–5 slices root ginger, peeled and shredded*	4–5 slices ginger root, peeled and shredded*
4 spring onions, cut into 2.5 cm/1 inch lengths	4 scallions, cut into 1 inch lengths
1 tablespoon sugar	1 tablespoon sugar
4 tablespoons soy sauce*	4 tablespoons soy sauce*
4 tablespoons wine vinegar	4 tablespoons wine vinegar
2 tablespoons dry sherry	2 tablespoons dry sherry

Cut the lobster halves into 3 or 4 pieces, depending on size. Rub all over with salt, monosodium glutamate, garlic, sherry and oil. Leave for 30 minutes.

Combine all the dip ingredients until well blended and pour into 2 small dishes.

Arrange the onions in the bottom of a large heatproof dish. Top with the lobster pieces. Place the dish in a steamer and steam vigorously for 9 to 10 minutes.

To serve, arrange the dip dishes on either side of the main dish with the lobster. SERVES 6 to 8.

Onion and Ginger Crab with Egg Sauce

SWEET AND SOUR WHOLE FISH

METRIC/IMPERIAL	AMERICAN
750 g–1 kg/1½–2 lb whole fish (trout, bream, carp, mullet, salmon etc.)	1½–2 lb whole fish (trout, bream, carp, mullet, salmon etc.)
2 teaspoons salt	2 teaspoons salt
1½ tablespoons vegetable oil	1½ tablespoons vegetable oil
3 tablespoons lard	3 tablespoons shortening
2 small chilli peppers, seeded and shredded	2 small chili peppers, seeded and shredded
6 spring onions, cut into 5 cm/2 inch lengths	6 scallions, cut into 2 inch lengths
6 slices root ginger, peeled and shredded*	6 slices ginger root, peeled and shredded*
1 red pepper, cored, seeded and shredded	1 red pepper, cored, seeded and shredded
2–3 pieces bamboo shoot, shredded*	2–3 pieces bamboo shoot, shredded*
3 tablespoons soy sauce*	3 tablespoons soy sauce*
3 tablespoons wine vinegar	3 tablespoons wine vinegar
1½ tablespoons sugar	1½ tablespoons sugar
1½ tablespoons tomato purée	1½ tablespoons tomato paste
3 tablespoons orange juice	3 tablespoons orange juice
1 tablespoon cornflour	1 tablespoon cornstarch
5 tablespoons clear stock	⅓ cup clear stock

Rub the fish inside and out with the salt and oil and leave for 30 minutes. Arrange the fish in an oval heatproof dish and place in a steamer. Steam vigorously for 15 minutes.

Heat the lard in a frying pan (skillet) over moderate heat. Add the chilli peppers and stir-fry for a few seconds. Add all the vegetables, the soy sauce, vinegar, sugar, tomato purée (paste) and orange juice. Stir-fry for a few seconds. Blend the cornflour (cornstarch) with the stock and add to the pan. Heat, stirring until the sauce thickens. To serve, arrange the fish on a platter and garnish with the vegetables from the frying pan (skillet). Pour the sauce over the fish.
SERVES 4.

Lobster with Bean Sprouts

STEAMED FIVE WILLOW FISH

METRIC/IMPERIAL	AMERICAN
750 g–1 kg/1½–2 lb whole fish (trout, bream, carp, mullet, salmon, etc.)	1½–2 lb whole fish (trout, bream, carp, mullet, salmon etc.)
2 teaspoons salt	2 teaspoons salt
1½ tablespoons vegetable oil	1½ tablespoons vegetable oil
3 tablespoons lard	3 tablespoons shortening
2 small chilli peppers, seeded and shredded	2 small chili peppers, seeded and shredded
6 spring onions, cut into 5 cm/2 inch lengths	6 scallions, cut into 2 inch lengths
6 slices root ginger, peeled and shredded*	6 slices ginger root, peeled and shredded*
1 red pepper, cored, seeded and shredded	1 red pepper, cored, seeded and shredded
2–3 pieces bamboo shoot, shredded*	2–3 pieces bamboo shoot, shredded*
3 tablespoons soy sauce*	3 tablespoons soy sauce*
3 tablespoons wine vinegar	3 tablespoons wine vinegar
1 tablespoon cornflour	1 tablespoon cornstarch
5 tablespoons clear stock	⅓ cup clear stock

Rub the fish inside and out with the salt and oil and leave for 30 minutes. Arrange the fish in an oval heatproof dish and place in a steamer. Steam vigorously for 15 minutes.

Heat the lard in a frying pan (skillet) over moderate heat. Add the chilli peppers and stir-fry for a few seconds. Add all the vegetables, the soy sauce and vinegar and stir-fry for 15 seconds. Blend the cornflour (cornstarch) with the stock and stir into the vegetables. Heat, stirring until the sauce thickens. To serve, arrange the fish on platter and garnish with the vegetables from the frying pan (skillet). Pour the sauce over the fish and serve immediately. SERVES 4.

Sweet and Sour Whole Fish

LOBSTER WITH BEAN SPROUTS

METRIC/IMPERIAL	AMERICAN
225 g/8 oz lobster meat, sliced	½ lobster meat, sliced
pinch of salt	pinch of salt
freshly ground black pepper	freshly ground black pepper
1 tablespoon vegetable oil	1 tablespoon vegetable oil
450 g/1 lb bean sprouts*	1 lb bean sprouts*
1 teaspoon cornflour	1 teaspoon cornstarch
1 teaspoon brown sugar	1 teaspoon brown sugar
3 tablespoons water	3 tablespoons water
1 tablespoon soy sauce*	1 tablespoon soy sauce*
1 spring onion, finely chopped	1 scallion, finely chopped

Season the lobster with salt and pepper. Heat the oil in a frying pan (skillet) and fry the lobster for 1 minute. Add the bean sprouts and stir-fry for 1 minute over a high heat.

Blend the cornflour (cornstarch), sugar, water and soy sauce to a smooth paste. Add to the pan and heat gently, stirring until slightly thickened. Add the spring onion (scallion) to the pan and mix well. Serve immediately. SERVES 4.

CRISPY SKIN FISH

METRIC/IMPERIAL	AMERICAN
3–4 slices root ginger, peeled and chopped*	3–4 slices ginger root, peeled and chopped*
1 tablespoon salt	1 tablespoon salt
750 g/1½ lb fish (whiting, herring, trout etc.)	1½ lb fish (whiting, herring, trout, etc.)
1½ tablespoons plain flour	1½ tablespoons all-purpose flour
oil for deep-frying	oil for deep-frying

Mix the ginger with the salt and rub over the fish, inside and out. Leave for 3 hours. Rub with the flour and leave for a further 30 minutes.

Heat the oil in a deep-fryer to 180°C/350°F. Arrange half the fish in a wire basket and deep-fry for 3 to 4 minutes, or until the fish are crisp and golden brown. Remove and keep hot. Deep-fry the remaining fish.

Return them all to the oil for a second frying for 2½ to 3 minutes, or until very crisp. Even the bones and heads of the fish should be crisp enough to eat. Serve immediately. SERVES 4 to 6.

SOLE WITH MUSHROOMS AND BAMBOO SHOOTS

METRIC/IMPERIAL	AMERICAN
1 tablespoon cornflour	1 tablespoon cornstarch
2 tablespoons soy sauce*	2 tablespoons soy sauce*
2 tablespoons dry sherry	2 tablespoons dry sherry
1 egg white	1 egg white
225 g/8 oz sole fillets, cut in to 3.5 cm/1½ inch strips	½ lb sole fillets, cut into 1½ inch strips
oil for deep-frying	oil for deep-frying
2 spring onions, finely chopped	2 scallions, finely chopped
50 g/2 oz mushrooms, thinly sliced	½ cup thinly sliced mushrooms
50 g/2 oz bamboo shoots, shredded*	½ cup shredded bamboo shoots*
1 small knob root ginger, peeled and shredded*	1 small knob ginger root, peeled and shredded*
2 tablespoons oil or lard	2 tablespoons oil or shortening
2 tablespoons water	2 tablespoons water
½ teaspoon monosodium glutamate*	½ teaspoon monosodium glutamate*

Blend the cornflour (cornstarch) to a smooth paste with the soy sauce and the sherry. Beat the egg white until frothy, then stir into the soy sauce mixture in a bowl. Toss the fish strips in the soy sauce mixture and leave for 10 minutes.

Heat the oil in a wok or deep-fryer to 180°C/350°F and deep-fry the fish strips for 2 to 3 minutes. Drain and keep hot. Heat the oil or lard in a frying pan (skillet) and stir-fry the spring onions (scallions), mushrooms, bamboo shoots and ginger for 1 minute over high heat.

Mix the water with the remaining soy mixture, stir into the pan with the monosodium glutamate. Heat gently, stirring until slightly thickened. Place the fish strips on a heated serving dish and pour the vegetables over. Serve immediately. SERVES 4.

CARP WITH SWEET AND SOUR SAUCE

METRIC/IMPERIAL	AMERICAN
15 g/½ oz dried wood ears, soaked in warm water for 30 minutes*	½ cup tree ears, soaked in warm water for 30 minutes*
1 × 750 g–1 kg/1½–2 lb carp	1 × 1½–2 lb carp
2 teaspoons salt	2 teaspoons salt
3 tablespoons flour	3 tablespoons flour
4 tablespoons vegetable oil	¼ cup vegetable oil
2–3 spring onions, shredded	2–3 scallions, shredded
2 slices root ginger, peeled and shredded*	2 slices ginger root, peeled and shredded*
1 garlic clove, peeled and finely chopped	1 garlic clove, peeled and finely chopped
15 g/½ oz bamboo shoots, thinly sliced*	2 tablespoons thinly sliced bamboo shoots*
50 g/2 oz water chestnuts, thinly sliced*	¼ cup thinly sliced water chestnuts*
1 red pepper, cored, seeded and shredded	1 red pepper, cored, seeded and shredded
3 tablespoons wine vinegar	3 tablespoons wine vinegar

Sauce:	Sauce:
3 tablespoons sugar	3 tablespoons sugar
2 tablespoons soy sauce*	2 tablespoons soy sauce*
2 tablespoons medium or dry sherry	2 tablespoons cream or pale dry sherry
2 teaspoons cornflour	2 teaspoons cornstarch
150 ml/¼ pint chicken stock or water	⅔ cup chicken stock or water
1 teaspoon chilli sauce	1 teaspoon chili sauce

Drain the wood (tree) ears and slice thinly, discarding the hard bits. Slash both sides of the fish diagonally to the bone at 5 mm/¼ inch intervals. Rub the fish inside and out with 1 teaspoon salt, then coat with the flour.

Heat the oil in a large wok or frying pan (skillet) until very hot. Lower the heat a little, add the fish and fry for 3 to 4 minutes on each side until golden and crisp, turning the fish carefully. Drain on kitchen paper towels then transfer to a warmed serving dish and keep hot.

Sole with Mushrooms and Bamboo Shoots; Carp with Sweet and Sour Sauce

Blend the sauce ingredients together until smooth. Put the spring onions (scallions), ginger and garlic in the pan. Stir in the wood (tree) ears, bamboo shoots, water chestnuts and red pepper, then the remaining salt and the vinegar. Add the sauce and heat, stirring, until it thickens. Pour over the fish. Serve immediately. SERVES 4.

23

SESAME FISH

METRIC/IMPERIAL	AMERICAN
1 onion, finely chopped	1 onion, finely chopped
1 teaspoon finely chopped root ginger*	1 teaspoon finely chopped ginger root*
2 tablespoons dry sherry	2 tablespoons dry sherry
½ teaspoon salt	½ teaspoon salt
pinch of freshly ground black pepper	pinch of freshly ground black pepper
1 teaspoon sugar	1 teaspoon sugar
450 g/1 lb fish fillets, cut in to bite-size pieces	1 lb fish fillets, cut into bite-size pieces
25 g/1 oz cornflour	2 tablespoons cornstarch
25 g/1 oz plain flour	¼ cup all-purpose flour
1 egg	1 egg
3 tablespoons water	3 tablespoons water
sesame seeds	sesame seeds
oil for deep-frying	oil for deep-frying

Mix together the onion, ginger, sherry, salt, pepper and sugar in a bowl. Add the fish pieces and marinate for 10 minutes, stirring occasionally. Drain.

Sift the cornflour (cornstarch) and flour into a bowl. Add the egg and water and mix to a smooth batter. Dip the fish into the batter and then into the sesame seeds.

Heat the oil in a wok or deep-fryer to 180°C/350°F and fry the fish pieces until crisp and golden. Drain and serve. SERVES 4.

FRIED LOBSTER WITH CABBAGE

METRIC/IMPERIAL	AMERICAN
2 tablespoons vegetable oil	2 tablespoons vegetable oil
1 small white cabbage, shredded	1 small white cabbage, shredded
½ teaspoon salt	½ teaspoon salt
6 tablespoons water	6 tablespoons water
450 g/1 lb lobster meat, cut into 2.5 cm/1 inch pieces	1 lb lobster meat, cut into 1 inch pieces
1 tablespoon soy sauce*	1 tablespoon soy sauce*
1 teaspoon sugar	1 teaspoon sugar
1 tablespoon medium or dry sherry	1 tablespoon cream or dry sherry
2 teaspoons cornflour	2 teaspoons cornstarch

Heat half the oil in a wok or frying pan (skillet). Add the cabbage and stir-fry for 1 minute over a high heat, stirring all the time. Add salt and 2 tablespoons water, cover and simmer for 2 to 3 minutes.

Heat the remaining oil in another frying pan (skillet) and stir-fry the lobster for 2 to 3 minutes. Add the soy sauce, sugar and sherry and stir well.

Blend the cornflour (cornstarch) to a smooth paste with the remaining water and add to the pan with the cabbage and its liquid, stirring until slightly thickened.

To serve, spoon the cabbage onto a warmed serving dish and pour the lobster mixture on top. SERVES 4.

FISH ROLLS WITH WALNUTS

METRIC/IMPERIAL	AMERICAN
2 spring onions, finely chopped	2 scallions, finely chopped
½ teaspoon salt	½ teaspoon salt
½ teaspoon sugar	½ teaspoon sugar
½ teaspoon cornflour	½ teaspoon cornstarch
1 teaspoon soy sauce*	1 teaspoon soy sauce*
1 teaspoon dry sherry	1 teaspoon dry sherry
1 egg	1 egg
2 large fish fillets (John Dory, plaice or sole), quartered	2 large fish fillets (flounder or sole), quartered
50 g/2 oz walnuts, finely chopped or ground	½ cup finely chopped or ground walnuts
2 slices cooked ham, quartered	2 slices cooked ham, quartered
8 wooden cocktail sticks	8 toothpicks
oil for deep-frying	oil for deep-frying

Mix the spring onions (scallions), salt, sugar, cornflour (cornstarch), soy sauce, sherry and egg and blend well together. Dip the fish pieces in the egg mixture and then into the walnuts. Lay a quarter slice of ham on each piece of fish. Roll up and secure with a cocktail stick (toothpick).

Heat the oil in a deep-fryer to 180°C/350°F and deep-fry the fish rolls until golden. Drain well on kitchen towels. Serve immediately. SERVES 4.

PINEAPPLE FISH

METRIC/IMPERIAL	AMERICAN
100 g/4 oz self-raising flour	1 cup self-raising flour
pinch of salt	pinch of salt
1 egg	1 egg
300 ml/½ pint water	1¼ cups water
pinch of monosodium glutamate*	pinch of monosodium glutamate*
450 g/1 lb haddock fillets, cut into bite-size pieces	1 lb haddock fillets, cut into bit-size pieces
oil for deep-frying	oil for deep-frying
2 tablespoons soft brown sugar	2 tablespoons light brown sugar
1 tablespoon cornflour	1 tablespoon cornstarch
2 tablespoons vinegar	2 tablespoons vinegar
1 tablespoon soy sauce*	1 tablespoon soy sauce*
1 teaspoon finely chopped root ginger*	1 teaspoon finely chopped ginger root*
150 ml/¼ pint syrup from canned pineapple	2/3 cup syrup from canned pineapple
salt	salt
4 pineapple rings, chopped	4 pineapple rings, chopped
toasted flaked almonds, to garnish	toasted flaked almonds, for garnish

Sift the flour and salt together in a mixing bowl. Make a well in the centre, add the egg, and mix with a little of the flour, using a wooden spoon. Gradually add half the water and draw in the flour. Beat until smooth, then beat in the monosodium glutamate.

Heat the oil in a wok or deep-fryer to 180°C/350°F. Dip the fish pieces in the batter and deep-fry until crisp and golden. Drain on kitchen paper towels and keep hot.

Fish Rolls with Walnuts; Golden Braised Fish

Blend together the brown sugar, cornflour (cornstarch), vinegar, soy sauce, ginger, pineapple syrup, salt and the remaing water. Bring to the boil, stirring, and boil for 2 or 3 minutes. Stir in the pineapple and heat through.

Arrange the fish in a hot bowl and sprinkle the almonds over the top. Serve with the sauce poured over. SERVES 4.

GOLDEN BRAISED FISH

METRIC/IMPERIAL	AMERICAN
1 kg/2 lb whole fish (bream or bass)	2 lb whole fish (bream or bass)
salt	salt
plain flour	all-purpose flour
4 Chinese dried mushrooms, soaked in warm water for 30 minutes*	4 Chinese dried mushrooms, soaked in warm water for 30 minutes*
oil for frying	oil for frying
4 spring onions, cut into 1 cm/½ inch lengths	4 scallions, cut into ½ inch lengths
1 teaspoon finely chopped root ginger*	1 teaspoon finely chopped ginger root*
300 ml/½ pint fish stock or water	1¼ cups fish stock or water
2 tablespoons soy sauce*	2 tablespoons soy sauce*
1 tablespoon dry sherry	1 tablespoon dry sherry
1 teaspoon salt	1 teaspoon salt
6 water chestnuts, sliced*	6 water chestnuts, sliced*
2 garlic cloves, crushed	2 garlic cloves, crushed
1 clove star anise*	1 clove star anise*
1 teaspoon sugar	1 teaspoon sugar

Clean the fish, leaving on the head and tail. Make 2 gashes on each side in the thickest part. Sprinkle with salt and coat with flour. Drain the mushrooms and slice thinly, discarding the stems.

Heat a little oil in a large frying pan (skillet) and fry fish on both sides until golden. Pour off the excess oil and add the mushrooms, spring onions (scallions), ginger, stock, soy sauce, sherry, salt, water chestnuts, garlic, star anise and sugar. Bring to the boil, cover and simmer for about 30 minutes, turning the fish once. Transfer the fish to a hot serving dish and spoon the vegetables and sauce over the top. SERVES 4.

GRILLED ORIENTAL FISH

METRIC/IMPERIAL	AMERICAN
2 tablespoons soy sauce*	2 tablespoons soy sauce*
2 slices root ginger, peeled and chopped*	2 slices ginger root, peeled and chopped*
¼ teaspoon five spice powder*	¼ teaspoon five spice powder*
2 tablespoons vegetable oil	2 tablespoons vegetable oil
pinch of sugar	pinch of sugar
pinch of freshly ground black pepper	pinch of freshly ground black pepper
2 tablespoons dry white wine	2 tablespoons dry white wine
6 thick white fish fillets	6 thick white fish fillets
coriander sprigs and spring onion tassels to garnish	coriander sprigs and scallion tassels for garnish

Combine the soy sauce, ginger, five spice powder, oil, sugar, pepper and wine in a flat dish. Place the fish in the dish and turn to coat. Leave to marinate for 1 hour, turning the fish once.

Line the grill (broiler) pan with foil, heat the grill (broiler) and place the fish in the pan skin side up. Pour over half the marinade and grill (broil) at high heat for 4 to 5 minutes. Pour on the remaining marinade and grill (broil) for a further 4 to 5 minutes.

Transfer to a heated serving dish and pour over any marinade remaining in the pan. Garnish with coriander sprigs and spring onions (scallion) tassels. SERVES 6.

BAKED RED-COOKED FISH

METRIC/IMPERIAL	AMERICAN
450–750 g/1–1½ lb fish (cod, haddock, carp, bream etc.), cut into 5–6 pieces	1–1½ lb fish (cod, haddock, carp, bream etc.), cut into 5–6 pieces
2 slices root ginger, peeled and chopped*	2 slices ginger root, peeled and chopped*
1 teaspoon salt	1 teaspoon salt
1 tablespoon soy sauce*	1 tablespoon soy sauce*
1 tablespoon hoisin sauce*	1 tablespoon hoisin sauce*
1½ tablespoons cornflour	1½ tablespoons cornstarch
1½ tablespoons vegetable oil	1½ tablespoons vegetable oil
Sauce:	Sauce:
3 spring onions, cut into 3.5 cm/1½ inch lengths	3 scallions, cut into 1½ inch lengths
1½ tablespoons lard	1½ tablespoons shortening
1½ tablespoons soy sauce*	1½ tablespoons soy sauce*
1½ tablespoons wine vinegar	1½ tablespoons wine vinegar
1½ tablespoons dry sherry	1½ tablespoons dry sherry
1½ teaspoons sugar	1½ teaspoons sugar

Arrange the fish pieces in a roasting pan. Rub the fish with the ginger, salt, soy sauce, hoisin sauce, cornflour (cornstarch) and oil and leave for 30 minutes.

Place the roasting pan in a preheated hot oven 220°C/425°F, Gas Mark 7 and cook for 10 to 12 minutes. Remove the fish pieces from the pan and arrange on a warmed serving dish.

Place the roasting pan over moderate heat. Add the sauce ingredients, stir and boil for 30 seconds. Pour the sauce over the fish and serve immediately. SERVES 4.

BASS WITH GINGER

METRIC/IMPERIAL	AMERICAN
1 kg/2 lb bass	2 lb bass
2 teaspoons salt	2 teaspoons salt
1 small knob root ginger, peeled and finely chopped*	1 small knob ginger root, peeled and finely chopped*
2 spring onions, finely chopped	2 scallions, finely chopped
1 tablespoon soy sauce*	1 tablespoon soy sauce*
1 teaspoon oil	1 teaspooon oil

Place the fish in a deep pan with the salt, cover with cold water and bring gently to the boil. Cover the pan and simmer for 5 minutes.

Mix together the ginger, spring onions (scallions), soy sauce and oil. Lift the fish from the pan, drain and place on a large serving dish. Pour the ginger mixture over and serve. SERVES 4.

STIR-FRIED BEAN CURD WITH CRAB

METRIC/IMPERIAL	AMERICAN
4 spring onions, finely chopped	4 scallions, finely chopped
1 teaspoon grated root ginger*	1 teaspoon grated ginger root*
225 g/8 oz crab meat	½ lb crab meat
2 tablespoons rice wine or dry sherry	2 tablespoons rice wine or dry sherry
450 ml/¾ pint chicken stock	2 cups chicken stock
2 teaspoons salt	2 teaspoons salt
1 teaspoon sesame seed oil*	1 teaspoon sesame seed oil*
¼ teaspoon freshly ground white pepper	¼ teaspoon freshly ground white pepper
2 tablespoons water	2 tablespoons water
1 tablespoon cornflour	1 tablespoon cornstarch
1 tablespoon peanut oil	1 tablespoon peanut oil
225 g/8 oz bean curd, cut into 2.5 cm/1 inch squares*	½ lb bean curd, cut into 1 inch squares*
2 egg whites, lightly beaten	2 egg whites, lightly beaten
2 spring onions, shredded, to garnish	2 scallions, shredded, for garnish

In a bowl mix the spring onions (scallions) and ginger together. Toss the crab meat with the wine. In another bowl mix the chicken stock, salt, sesame oil and pepper. Blend the water and cornflour (cornstarch) to a smooth paste.

Heat the peanut oil in a wok or heavy frying pan (skillet) over high heat. Add spring onion mixture and stir-fry for 3 seconds. Add stock mixture and bean curd, bring to the boil, add the crab meat and wine, then turn down the heat and cook for 5 minutes.

Add the cornflour (cornstarch) mixture to the pan, stirring carefully to avoid breaking the bean curd. Simmer for 1 minute. Add the egg whites in a stream, rotating the pan. To serve arrange the contents of the pan in a hot serving bowl and sprinkle with shredded spring onion (scallion). SERVES 6.

Grilled Oriental Fish; Baked Red-Cooked Fish

Poultry

CHICKEN WINGS AND BROCCOLI ASSEMBLY

METRIC/IMPERIAL	AMERICAN
12 chicken wings, trimmed and cut into 2 pieces	12 chicken wings, trimmed and cut into 2 pieces
4 spring onions, finely chopped	4 scallions, finely chopped
2 slices root ginger, peeled and finely chopped*	2 slices ginger root, peeled and finely chopped*
1 tablespoon lemon juice	1 tablespoon lemon juice
1 tablespoon soy sauce*	1 tablespoon soy sauce*
1½ teaspoons salt	1½ teaspoons salt
1 tablespoon medium or dry sherry	1 tablespoon cream or pale dry sherry
4 tablespoons vegetable oil	¼ cup vegetable oil
225 g/8 oz broccoli, divided into florets	½ lb broccoli, divided into florets
50 g/2 oz tomatoes, chopped	¼ cup chopped tomatoes
1 tablespoon cornflour	1 tablespoon cornstarch
2 tablespoons water	2 tablespoons water

Place the chicken in a bowl with the spring onions (scallions), ginger, lemon juice, soy sauce, ½ teaspoon salt and the sherry. Stir well, then leave to marinate for 20 minutes.

Heat 2 tablespoons of vegetable oil in a wok or frying pan (skillet). Add the broccoli and remaining salt and stir-fry until tender but still crisp. Arrange the broccoli around the edge of a warmed serving dish and keep hot.

Remove the chicken pieces, reserving the marinade. Heat the remaining oil in the pan, add the chicken and fry until golden. Remove with a slotted spoon and drain.

Add the tomatoes to the pan and stir-fry until reduced to a pulp. Return the chicken to the pan with the marinade and cook for 2 minutes. Blend the cornflour (cornstarch) with the water and add to the pan. Heat, stirring constantly, until thickened. Spoon the chicken and sauce into the centre of the serving dish and serve immediately. SERVES 6.

SWEET CHICKEN WINGS WITH OYSTER SAUCE

METRIC/IMPERIAL	AMERICAN
450 g/1 lb chicken wings	1 lb chicken wings
3 tablespoons oyster sauce*	3 tablespoons oyster sauce*
1 tablespoon soy sauce*	1 tablespoon soy sauce*
300 ml/½ pint chicken stock	1¼ cups chicken stock
pinch of salt	pinch of salt
1 teaspoon brown sugar	1 teaspoon brown sugar
25 g/1 oz ginger root, finely chopped*	1 oz ginger root, finely chopped*
freshly ground black pepper	freshly ground black pepper
1 teaspoon coarse salt	1 teaspoon coarse salt

Wash and dry the chicken wings and place in a large pan. Cover with cold water. Bring to the boil, cover and simmer for 10 minutes then drain.

Place the chicken wings in a clean pan and add the oyster sauce, soy sauce, chicken stock, salt and sugar. Bring gently to the boil, lower and simmer for 20 minutes. Transfer to a hot serving dish and sprinkle the ginger, salt and pepper over the chicken. SERVES 4.

BRAISED CHICKEN WINGS

METRIC/IMPERIAL	AMERICAN
4 Chinese dried mushroom, soaked in warm water for 30 minutes*	4 Chinese dried mushrooms, soaked in warm water for 30 minutes*
2 tablespoons vegetable oil	2 tablespoons vegetable oil
2 spring onions, finely chopped	2 scallions, finely chopped
2 slices root ginger, peeled and finely chopped*	2 slices ginger root, peeled and finely chopped*
12 chicken wings, trimmed and each cut into 2 pieces	12 chicken wings, trimmed and each cut into 2 pieces
2 tablespoons soy sauce*	2 tablespoons soy sauce*
2 tablespoons medium or dry sherry	2 tablespoons cream or pale dry sherry
1 tablespoon sugar	1 tablespoon sugar
½ teaspoon five spice powder*	½ teaspoon five spice powder*
350 ml/12 fl oz water	1½ cups water
175 g/6 oz bamboo shoots, cut into chunks*	1½ cups bamboo shoots, cut into chunks*
2 teaspoons cornflour	2 teaspoons cornstarch
1 tablespoon cold water	1 tablespoon cold water

Drain the mushrooms, squeeze dry, discard stems and cut caps into small pieces. Heat the oil in a wok or frying pan (skillet) until it reaches smoking point, then add the spring onions (scallions), ginger and chicken wings. Stir-fry until the chicken changes colour, then add the soy sauce, sherry, sugar, five spice powder and water.

Lower the heat and cook gently until the liquid has reduced by about half. Add the mushrooms and bamboo shoots and continue cooking until the liquid has almost completely evaporated. Remove the bamboo chunks with a slotted spoon, rinse and drain, and arrange around the edge of a warmed serving dish.

Blend the cornflour (cornstarch) with the cold water, then add to the pan and cook, stirring constantly, until thickened. Place the chicken mixture in the centre of the bamboo shoots and serve hot. SERVES 6.

Braised Chicken Wings; Chicken Wings and Broccoli Assembly

SHREDDED CHICKEN WITH FISH SAUCE

METRIC/IMPERIAL	AMERICAN
350 g/12 oz chicken breast meat, shredded	1½ cups shredded chicken breast meat
½ teaspoon salt	½ teaspoon salt
½ egg white	½ egg white
1 teaspoon cornflour	1 teaspoon cornstarch
4 tablespoons vegetable oil	¼ cup vegetable oil
2 spring onions, cut into 2.5 cm/1 inch lengths	2 scallions, cut into 1 inch lengths
1 slice root ginger, peeled and shredded*	1 slice ginger root, peeled and shredded*
1 small green pepper, cored, seeded and cut into rings	1 small green pepper, cored, seeded and cut into rings
1 small red pepper, cored, seeded and cut into rings	1 small red pepper, cored, seeded and cut into rings
3 celery sticks, sliced	3 celery stalks, sliced
1 tablespoon soy sauce*	1 tablespoon soy sauce*
1 teaspoon sugar	1 teaspoon sugar
1 teaspoon vinegar	1 teaspoon vinegar
1 teaspoon chilli sauce (optional)	1 teaspoon chili sauce (optional)

Place the chicken in a bowl with the salt, egg white and cornflour (cornstarch). Mix well and leave for 20 minutes.

Heat 2 tablespoons oil in a wok or frying pan (skillet), add the chicken and stir-fry for 2 minutes. Remove from the pan with a slotted spoon and drain.

Heat the remaining oil in the pan and add the spring onions (scallions), ginger, peppers and celery. Stir in the soy sauce, sugar, vinegar and chilli sauce, if using. Return the chicken to the pan and combine all the ingredients together. Transfer to a hot serving dish. SERVES 4.

STEAMED CHICKEN WITH CHINESE DRIED MUSHROOMS

METRIC/IMPERIAL	AMERICAN
450 g/1 lb boned chicken meat, cut into small pieces	1 lb boned chicken meat, cut into small pieces
1½ tablespoons soy sauce*	1½ tablespoons soy sauce*
1 tablespoon medium or dry sherry	1 tablespoon cream or pale dry sherry
1 teaspoon sugar	1 teaspoon sugar
1 teaspoon cornflour	1 teaspoon cornstarch
4 Chinese dried mushrooms, soaked in warm water for 30 minutes*	4 Chinese dried mushrooms, soaked in warm water for 30 minutes*
1 tablespoon vegetable oil	1 tablespoon vegetable oil
2 slices root ginger, peeled and shredded*	2 slices ginger root, peeled and shredded*
freshly ground black pepper	freshly ground black pepper
1 teaspoon sesame seed oil*	1 teaspoon sesame seed oil*

Place the chicken in a bowl with the soy sauce, sherry, sugar and cornflour (cornstarch). Mix well, then leave to marinate for 20 minutes. Drain the mushrooms.

Brush a heatproof plate with the vegetable oil. Place the chicken on the plate, top with the mushrooms, then sprinkle with the ginger, pepper and sesame seed oil. Place in a steamer or over a pan of simmering water and cover the plate with a lid. Steam over high heat for 25 to 30 minutes. Transfer to a hot serving dish and serve immediately. SERVES 4.

Shredded Chicken with Fish Sauce; Steamed Chicken with Chinese Dried Mushrooms; Golden Flower and Jade Tree Chicken

GOLDEN FLOWER AND JADE TREE CHICKEN

METRIC/IMPERIAL	AMERICAN
1 × 1.5 kg/3–3½ lb chicken	1 × 3–3½ lb broiler/fryer
2 slices root ginger, peeled*	2 slices ginger root, peeled*
2 spring onions	2 scallions
3 tablespoons vegetable oil	3 tablespoons vegetable oil
450 g/1 lb broccoli or other green vegetable, divided into florets or small pieces	1 lb broccoli or other green vegetable, divided into florets or small pieces
2 teaspoons salt	2 teaspoons salt
250 ml/8 fl oz chicken stock	1 cup chicken stock or broth
225 g/8 oz cooked ham	½ lb cooked ham
1 tablespoon cornflour	1 tablespoon cornstarch
2 tablespoons water	2 tablespoons water

Place the chicken in a large pan and cover with cold water. Add the ginger and spring onions (scallions), cover with a tight-fitting lid and bring to the boil. Lower the heat and simmer for exactly 3 minutes. Turn off the heat and leave the chicken to cook in the hot water for at least 3 hours, without removing the lid.

Heat the oil in a wok or frying pan (skillet). Add the broccoli or greens and 1 teaspoon salt, then stir-fry for 3 to 4 minutes, moistening with a little stock if necessary. Remove the vegetables from the pan and arrange around the edge of a large serving dish.

Remove the chicken from the pan and carefully remove the meat from the bones, leaving on the skin. Cut the chicken and ham into thin rectangular slices and arrange in alternating overlapping layers in the centre of the broccoli.

Just before serving, heat the remaining stock with the remaining salt in a small pan. Blend the cornflour (cornstarch) with the water and add to the stock. Heat, stirring, until thickened. Pour over the chicken and ham to form a thin glaze, resembling jade. Serve hot. SERVES 6 to 8.

FRIED CHICKEN LEGS

METRIC/IMPERIAL	AMERICAN
6 chicken legs, each chopped into 2–3 pieces	6 chicken legs, each chopped into 2–3 pieces
2 tablespoons soy sauce*	2 tablespoons soy sauce*
1 tablespoon medium or dry sherry	1 tablespoon cream or pale dry sherry
½ teaspoon freshly ground black pepper	½ teaspoon freshly ground black pepper
2 tablespoons cornflour	2 tablespoons cornstarch
600 ml/1 pint vegetable oil for deep-frying	2½ cups vegetable oil for deep-frying
1 tablespoon finely chopped spring onion	1 tablespoon finely chopped scallion

Mix the chicken legs with the soy sauce, sherry and pepper. Leave to marinate for 20 minutes, turning occasionally.

Coat each piece of chicken with cornflour (cornstarch). Heat the oil in a wok or deep-fryer to 180°C/350°F. Lower the heat, add the chicken pieces and deep-fry until golden. Remove from the pan with a slotted spoon and drain.

Pour off all but 1 tablespoon oil and add the spring onion (scallion) to the pan with the chicken pieces. Stir-fry over a moderate heat for about 2 minutes. Transfer to a hot serving dish and serve immediately. SERVES 6.

LOTUS-WHITE CHICKEN

METRIC/IMPERIAL	AMERICAN
5 egg whites	5 egg whites
120 ml/4 fl oz chicken stock	½ cup chicken stock or broth
1 teaspoon salt	1 teaspoon salt
1 teaspoon medium or dry sherry	1 teaspoon cream or pale dry sherry
2 teaspoons cornflour	2 teaspoons cornstarch
100 g/4 oz chicken breast meat, finely chopped	½ cup finely chopped chicken breast meat
oil for deep-frying	oil for deep-frying
To garnish:	For garnish:
1–2 tablespoons cooked green peas	1–2 tablespoons cooked green peas
25 g/1 oz cooked ham, shredded	2 tablespoons shredded cooked ham

Place the egg whites in a bowl. Stir in 3 tablespoons of the chicken stock, the salt, sherry and 1 teaspoon cornflour (cornstarch). Add the chicken and mix well.

Heat the oil in a wok or deep-fryer to 180°C/350°F then gently pour in one third of the mixture. Deep-fry for 10 seconds until the mixture begins to rise to the surface, then carefully turn over. Deep-fry until golden, then remove with a slotted spoon and drain. Keep hot on a warmed serving dish and cook the remainder of the mixture in the same way.

Heat the remaining stock in a small pan. Mix the remaining cornflour (cornstarch) to a paste with a little cold water, add to the stock and heat, stirring, until thickened. Pour over the chicken. Garnish with the peas and ham and serve hot. SERVES 4.

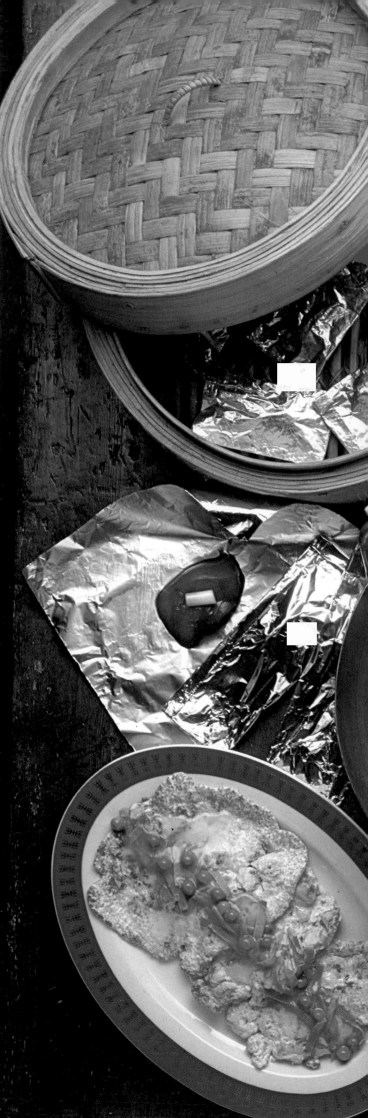

CHICKEN IN SILVER FOIL

METRIC/IMPERIAL	AMERICAN
450 g/1 lb skinned chicken breast meat, cut into 12 pieces	1 lb skinned chicken breast meat, cut into 12 pieces
3 spring onions, white part only, quartered	3 scallions, white part only, quartered
¼ teaspoon salt	¼ teaspoon salt
1 tablespoon soy sauce*	1 tablespoon soy sauce*
1 teaspoon sugar	1 teaspoon sugar
1 teaspoon medium or dry sherry	1 teaspoon cream or pale dry sherry
1 teaspoon sesame seed oil*	1 teaspoon sesame seed oil*
4 tablespoons vegetable oil	¼ cup oil
To garnish:	For garnish:
shredded spring onion	shredded scallion
finely chopped red pepper	finely chopped red pepper

Put the chicken and spring onions (scallions) into a bowl with the salt, soy sauce, sugar, sherry and sesame seed oil. Leave to marinate for 20 minutes.

Cut 12 squares of foil large enough to wrap round the chicken pieces 4 times. Brush the foil with oil then place 1 piece of chicken on each. Top with a piece of spring onion (scallion), then wrap the foil around the chicken to make a parcel, making sure no meat is exposed.

Heat the oil in a wok or frying pan (skillet). Add the chicken parcels and fry over moderate heat for 2 minutes on each side. Remove and drain.

Reheat the oil. When it is very hot, return the chicken parcels to the pan and fry for 1 minute only. Serve hot in the silver foil, garnished with shredded spring onion (scallion) and red pepper. SERVES 4.

WHITE-CUT CHICKEN

METRIC/IMPERIAL	AMERICAN
1 × 1.5 kg/3–3½ lb chicken	1 × 3½ lb chicken
2–3 spring onions, finely chopped	2–3 scallions, finely chopped
2 slices of fresh root ginger*, peeled and chopped	2 slices of fresh ginger root*, peeled and finely chopped
1 teaspoon salt	1 teaspoon salt
1 tablespoon soy sauce	1 tablespoon soy sauce
1 tablespoon sesame seed oil*	1 tablespoon sesame seed oil*
freshly ground black pepper	freshly ground black pepper

Put the chicken in a large pan, add cold water to cover, then cover the pan with a tight-fitting lid. Bring to the boil, lower the heat and simmer for 7 minutes. Turn off the heat and leave until cool. One hour before serving, remove the chicken from the water and chop it into small pieces. Arrange on a serving dish.

Mix together the sauce ingredients and pour over the chicken. Cover and leave in the refrigerator for at least 30 minutes before serving. SERVES 4.

Chicken in Silver Foil; Fried Chicken Legs; Lotus-White Chicken

DICED CHICKEN WITH CELERY

METRIC/IMPERIAL	AMERICAN
3–4 Chinese dried mushrooms, soaked in warm water for 30 minutes*	3–4 Chinese dried mushrooms, soaked in warm water for 30 minutes*
225 g/8 oz chicken breast meat, skinned and diced	1 cup diced, skinned chicken meat
½ teaspoon salt	½ teaspoon salt
1 egg white	1 egg white
1 tablespoon cornflour	1 tablespoon cornstarch
5 tablespoons vegetable oil	⅓ cup vegetable oil
2 slices root ginger, peeled and finely chopped*	2 slices ginger root, peeled and finely chopped*
2–3 spring onions, finely chopped	2–3 scallions, finely chopped
1 small celery head, diced	1 small celery bunch, diced
100 g/4 oz bamboo shoots, diced*	1 cup diced bamboo shoots*
1 red pepper, cored, seeded and diced	1 red pepper, cored, seeded and diced
3 tablespoons soy sauce*	3 tablespoons soy sauce*
1 teaspoon medium or dry sherry	1 teaspoon cream or pale dry sherry
chopped coriander leaves or parsley, to garnish	chopped coriander leaves or parsley, for garnish

Drain the mushrooms, squeeze dry, discard the stems and dice the caps. Sprinkle the chicken with the salt, dip into the egg white then coat with the cornflour (cornstarch).

Heat the oil in a wok or frying pan (skillet). Add the chicken, stir-fry over moderate heat until half-cooked, then remove with a slotted spoon.

Increase the heat to high and add the ginger and spring onions (scallions) to the pan. Add the mushrooms and remaining vegetables and stir-fry for 1 minute.

Return the chicken to the pan, add the soy sauce and sherry and cook for a further minute until the liquid thickens, stirring constantly. Serve hot, garnished with chopped coriander or parsley. SERVES 4.

PAPER (PARCHMENT) WRAPPED CHICKEN

METRIC/IMPERIAL	AMERICAN
2 spring onions, finely chopped	2 scallions, finely chopped
25 g/1 oz root ginger, peeled and chopped*	1 tablespoon peeled and chopped ginger root*
2 tablespoons soy sauce*	2 tablespoons soy sauce*
1 tablespoon sherry	1 tablespoon sherry
pinch of brown sugar	pinch of brown sugar
pinch of salt	pinch of salt
pinch of freshly ground black pepper	pinch of freshly ground black pepper
450 g/1 lb chicken meat, cut into 16 slices	1 lb chicken meat, cut into 16 slices
oil for deep-frying	oil for deep-frying

Mix together the spring onions (scallions), ginger, soy sauce, sherry, sugar, salt and pepper. Toss the chicken slices in the soy sauce mixture. Leave covered for 30 minutes.

Cut 16 squares of greaseproof (waxed) paper or non-stick parchment. Wrap each piece of chicken in a piece of paper or parchment and secure. Heat the oil in a wok or deep-fryer to 180°C/350°F and deep-fry the parcels for 3 minutes. Drain and serve hot. SERVES 4.

PAN-FRIED CHICKEN BREAST

METRIC/IMPERIAL	AMERICAN
1 large chicken breast, skinned, boned and cut into thin slices	1 large chicken breast, skinned, boned and cut into thin slices
1–2 spring onions, chopped	1–2 scallions, chopped
1 slice root ginger, peeled and finely chopped*	1 slice ginger root, peeled and finely chopped*
1 tablespoon medium or dry sherry	1 tablespoon cream or pale dry sherry
2 teaspoons salt	2 teaspoons salt
1 egg, beaten	1 egg, beaten
2 teaspoons cornflour	3 teaspoons cornstarch
3 tablespoons vegetable oil	3 teaspoons vegetable oil
1 small lettuce	1 small head lettuce
Sauce:	Sauce:
1 tablespoon tomato purée	1 tablespoon tomato paste
1 teaspoon sugar	1 teaspoon sugar
1 teaspoon sesame seed oil*	1 teaspoon sesame seed oil*
1 tablespoon water	1 tablespoon water

Place the chicken slices in a bowl. Add the spring onion (scallion), ginger, sherry and salt and mix well. Leave to marinate for 20 minutes.

Stir the egg into the marinated chicken, then sprinkle with the cornflour (cornstarch) and toss to coat thoroughly.

Heat the oil in a wok or frying pan (skillet). Add the chicken slices and fry until tender and golden on all sides. Remove from the pan with a slotted spoon and arrange on a bed of lettuce.

Mix the sauce ingredients together. Add to the pan in which the chicken was cooked and heat through. Pour the sauce over the chicken or, if preferred, serve separately as a dip. SERVES 4.

SWEET AND SOUR CHICKEN DRUMSTICKS

METRIC/IMPERIAL	AMERICAN
6 chicken drumsticks	6 chicken drumsticks
1 egg	1 egg
1 tablespoon water	1 tablespoon water
5 tablespoons cornflour	5 tablespoons cornstarch
salt	salt
freshly ground black pepper	freshly ground black pepper
1 onion, cut into chunks	1 onion, cut into chunks
1 small pepper, cored, seeded and sliced	1 small pepper, cored, seeded and sliced

1 carrot, cut into wedges
450 ml/¾ pint chicken stock
4 tablespoons vinegar
4 tablespoons soft brown sugar
1 tablespoon soy sauce*
1 tablespoon medium or dry
  sherry
oil for deep-frying

1 carrot, cut into wedges
2 cups chicken stock
4 tablespoons vinegar
¼ cup firmly packed light
  brown sugar
1 tablespoon soy sauce*
1 tablespoon cream or pale dry
  sherry
oil for deep-frying

Diced Chicken with Celery; Pan-Fried Chicken Breast

Put the onion and carrot pieces in a small saucepan of boiling water and cook for 5 minutes. Drain well. Blend together the chicken stock, vinegar, sugar, remaining cornflour (cornstarch), soy sauce and sherry in a small saucepan. Bring to the boil, stirring constantly, and simmer for 2 to 3 minutes.

Heat the oil in a deep frying pan (skillet) and fry the drumsticks until golden and tender. Drain on kitchen paper towels. Add the vegetables to the sauce together with the chicken and reheat. Arrange on a hot serving dish and serve immediately. SERVES 6.

Trim the drumsticks if necessary. Beat the egg with the water. Mix 4 tablespoons cornflour (cornstarch) with salt and pepper. Dip the drumsticks in the egg, then in the seasoned cornflour (cornstarch) and leave aside.

35

PEKING DUCK

METRIC/IMPERIAL

1 × 2 kg/4½ lb duck
1 tablespoon dark brown sugar
1 tablespoon soy sauce*
300 ml/½ pint water
4–5 spring onions, cut into 5
  cm/2 inch lengths
½ medium cucumber, shredded
Sauce:
2 tablespoons soy sauce*
1¼ tablespoons soy paste*
1¼ tablespoons hoisin sauce*
1¼ tablespoons sugar
2 tablespoons plum sauce*
1 tablespoon sesame seed oil*
pancakes, to serve (see below)

AMERICAN

1 × 4½ lb duck
1 tablespoon firmly packed
  dark brown sugar
1 tablespoon soy sauce*
1¼ cups water
4–5 scallions, cut into 2 inch
  lengths
½ medium cucumber, shredded
Sauce:
2 tablespoons soy sauce*
1¼ tablespoons soy paste*
1¼ tablespoons hoisin sauce*
1¼ tablespoons sugar
2 tablespoons plum sauce*
1 tablespoon sesame seed oil*
crêpes to serve (see below)

Scald the skin of the duck with a large kettleful of boiling water, turning the duck over once. Pat the skin dry with kitchen paper towels. Hang the duck up by the neck to dry overnight in an airy place. Mix together the brown sugar, soy sauce and water until well blended. Brush the duck with this mixture and leave to dry for 30 minutes. Combine all the sauce ingredients until well blended.

Place the duck on a rack in a roasting pan. Place in an oven preheated to 190°C/375°F, Gas Mark 5. Roast for 1 hour without basting or opening the oven door. After 1 hour the duck should be cooked and the skin crispy.

Put the sauce mixture in a saucepan and cook for 2 minutes, stirring constantly.

To serve, carve the skin of the duck into 4 x 2.5 cm/1 inch pieces and spread out on a warmed serving dish. Carve the meat into similar-sized pieces and place on a separate dish. To eat, brush a pancake with sauce, top with 1 or 2 pieces of spring onions (scallions) and shredded cucumber, a slice of skin and a slice of meat. The pancake is then rolled up and eaten with the fingers. SERVES 6 to 8.

PANCAKES (CRÊPES)

METRIC/IMPERIAL

225 g/8 oz plain flour
250 ml/8 fl oz boiling water
2 tablespoons sesame seed oil*

AMERICAN

2 cups all-purpose flour
1 cup boiling water
2 tablespoons sesame seed oil*

Sift the flour into a bowl. Slowly pour the boiling water on to the flour, beating constantly with a wooden spoon until the mixture forms a dough. Knead the dough for 5 to 6 minutes, then rest the dough for 10 minutes. Form the dough into a long roll about 5 cm/2 inches in diameter. Cut the roll into 1 cm/½ inch slices. Roll the slices into 15 cm/6 inch diameter pancakes (crêpes). Brush the top of 2 pancakes with sesame seed oil and place on top of each other, the oiled slices facing inwards. Sandwich the remaining pancakes in the same way.

Place a heavy, ungreased frying pan (skillet) over a moderate heat. When hot, place a double pancake on the pan and heat for about 3 minutes each side. (Brown spots will appear and some parts of the pancake will start to bubble when it is cooked.) Remove the pancake from the pan and cool a little.

Pull the pancakes apart into two. Fold each one across the centre, on the greased side. Stack on a heatproof dish and place in a steamer. Steam for 10 minutes and serve.

The pancakes will keep in the refrigerator for 2 to 3 days and should be steamed again for 7 to 8 minutes before serving. MAKES 10 to 12.

Peking Duck

BRAISED CHICKEN WITH PEPPERS

METRIC/IMPERIAL	AMERICAN
3 tablespoons vegetable oil	3 tablespoons vegetable oil
1 teaspoon salt	1 teaspoon salt
3 red peppers, cored, sliced and cut into rings	3 red peppers, cored, seeded and cut into rings
2 tablespoons water	2 tablespoons water
450 g/1 lb chicken meat, cut into 2.5 cm/1 inch pieces	1 lb chicken meat, cut into 1 inch pieces
25 g/1 oz root ginger, peeled and finely chopped*	1 tablespoon peeled and finely chopped ginger root*
pinch of brown sugar	pinch of brown sugar
2 teaspoons medium or dry sherry	2 teaspoons cream or pale dry sherry
1 teaspoon cornflour	1 teaspoon cornstarch
2 teaspoons soy sauce*	2 teaspoons soy sauce*

Heat 1 tablespoon of oil with the salt in a wok or frying pan (skillet). Stir-fry the peppers for 1 minute. Add the water, bring to the boil, cover and simmer for 2 minutes. Drain and reserve.

Heat the remaining oil in the wok or frying pan (skillet) and stir-fry the chicken and ginger for 1 minute. Add the sugar and sherry and mix well. Mix the cornflour (cornstarch) to a smooth paste with the soy sauce and add to the pan. Heat gently, stirring until slightly thickened. Add the peppers and cook for 1 minute. Serve hot. SERVES 6.

SHREDDED DUCK QUICK-FRIED WITH SHREDDED GINGER

METRIC/IMPERIAL	AMERICAN
½ teaspoon salt	½ teaspoon salt
2 tablespoons soy sauce*	2 tablespoons soy sauce*
1 tablespoon soy paste or hoisin sauce*	1 tablespoon soy paste of hoisin sauce*
2 tablespoons dry sherry	2 tablespoons dry sherry
5–6 slices root ginger, peeled and shredded*	5–6 slices ginger root, peeled and shredded*
450 g/1 lb duck meat, cut into matchstick strips	1 lb duck meat, cut into matchstick strips
2½ tablespoons vegetable oil	2½ tablespoons vegetable oil
1 tablespoon lard	1 tablespoon lard
3 spring onions, cut into 3.5 cm/1½ inch lengths	3 scallions, cut into 1½ inch lengths
1 tablespoon cornflour	1 tablespoon cornstarch
3 tablespoons water	3 tablespoons water

In a bowl mix together the salt, soy sauce, soy paste, sherry and ginger, then add the duck meat. Stir and turn until well blended and leave for 30 minutes.

Heat the oil in a wok or frying pan (skillet) over a high heat. Add the meat and ginger mixture and stir-fry for 2 minutes. Add the lard. When the fat has melted, sprinkle over the spring onions (scallions).

Blend the cornflour (cornstarch) with the water and add to the pan. Stir and turn for 1 minute then transfer to a warmed serving dish. SERVES 4 to 6.

ONION AND LEEK WINE-SIMMERED DUCK

METRIC/IMPERIAL	AMERICAN
6 medium Chinese dried mushrooms, soaked in 300 ml/½ pint warm water for 30 minutes*	6 medium Chinese dried mushrooms, soaked in 1¼ cups warm water for 30 minutes*
5 tablespoons vegetable oil	⅓ cup vegetable oil
4 medium onions, halved	4 medium onions, halved
1 × 2–2.25 kg/4½–5 lb duck	1 × 4½–5 lb duck
4 slices root ginger, peeled and chopped*	4 slices ginger root, peeled and chopped*
1 teaspoon salt	1 teaspoon salt
4 tablespoons soy sauce*	4 tablespoons soy sauce*
900 ml/1½ pints water	3¾ cups water
300 ml/½ pint red wine	1¼ cups red wine
1 chicken stock cube	2 chicken bouillon cubes
2 small leeks, cut into 5 cm/ 2 inch lengths	2 small leeks, cut into 2 inch lengths

Drain the mushrooms and squeeze dry, reserving the soaking liquid. Discard the stems and cut the caps into quarters. Heat the oil in a frying pan (skillet) and sauté the onions for 4 or 5 minutes. Drain. Fry the duck in the same oil for 5 to 6 minutes until lightly browned. Stuff the cavity of the duck with the ginger, salt, onions and mushrooms.

Place the duck in a heavy saucepan or flameproof casserole. Add 2 tablespoons soy sauce and the water. Bring to the boil, cover and simmer gently for 45 minutes, turning the duck once. Leave to cool. When it is cold, skim off any skum from the surface. Discard two thirds of the liquid. Add the wine, reserved mushroom soaking liquid, remaining soy sauce and crumbled stock cube (bouillon cube). Bring to the boil, cover and simmer gently for 1 hour, or until the liquid is reduced by half, turning the duck twice.

Remove the duck and arrange in a deep warmed serving dish. Add the leeks to the casserole, increase the heat to high and boil rapidly until the liquid is reduced by half. Spoon the sauce from the casserole over the duck and arrange the leeks around it. SERVES 4 to 6.

CRYSTAL DUCK WITH CHRYSANTHEMUMS

METRIC/IMPERIAL	AMERICAN
1 × 1.5–2 kg/3½–4½ lb duck, chopped into 12–15 pieces	1 × 3½–4½ lb duck, chopped into 12–15 pieces
1 tablespoon salt	1 tablespoon salt
4 slices root ginger, peeled and chopped*	4 slices ginger root, peeled and chopped*
2 medium onions, halved	2 medium onions, halved
900 ml/1½ pints clear stock	3¾ cups clear stock or broth
300 ml/½ pint white wine	1¼ cups white wine
1 small envelope gelatine	1 small envelope unflavored gelatin
3 spring onions, cut into 5 cm/2 inch lengths	3 scallions, cut into 2 inch lengths
225 g/8 oz smoked ham, chopped into 5 cm/2 inch lengths	½ lb smoked ham, chopped into 2 inch lengths
1 large chrysanthemum	1 large chrysanthemum
8 small chrysanthemums	8 small chrysanthemums

Place the duck pieces in a flameproof casserole. Add the salt, ginger and onions. Pour in the stock and 150 ml/¼ pint/⅔ cup wine. Bring to the boil. Place the casserole in a preheated moderate oven, 180°C/350°F, Gas Mark 4 for 1½ hours, stirring every 30 minutes.

Remove the casserole from the oven and discard the onion and ginger. Pour the liquid into a separate pan, add the gelatine and stir until it has dissolved. Add the remaining wine. Skim off any scum from the surface and pour the liquid through fine muslin or cheesecloth to obtain a clear consommé.

Arrange the duck pieces, skin side down, in a heatproof glass dish. Decorate with the spring onions (scallions), ham and petals from the large chrysanthemum. Pour the consommé over them and place the dish in the oven to heat through for a further 15 minutes. Remove the dish from the oven. Leave to cool for 1 hour, then place in the refrigerator for 3 to 4 hours, or until set.

To serve, unmould the duck onto a dish and decorate with the 8 small chrysanthemums. SERVES 6 to 8.

Onion and Leek Wine-Simmered Duck

CANTONESE ROAST DUCK

METRIC/IMPERIAL	AMERICAN
3 garlic cloves, crushed	3 garlic cloves, crushed
1 medium onion, thinly sliced	1 medium onion, thinly sliced
½ teaspoon five spice powder*	½ teaspoon five spice powder*
2 teaspoons sugar	2 teaspoons sugar
5 tablespoons clear stock	⅓ cup clear stock
1½ tablespoons soy sauce*	1½ tablespoons soy sauce*
1½ tablespoons soy paste*	1½ tablespoons soy paste*
3 tablespoons medium or dry sherry	3 tablespoons cream or pale dry sherry
1 × 2 kg/4½ lb duck	1 × 4½ lb duck
Skin coating:	Skin coating:
300 ml/½ pint water	1¼ cups water
4–5 tablespoons clear honey	4–5 tablespoons clear honey
5 tablespoons wine vinegar	⅓ cup wine vinegar
2 tablespoons soy sauce*	2 tablespoons soy sauce*

Mix the garlic, onion, five spice powder, sugar, stock, soy sauce, soy paste and sherry together until well blended. Spoon the mixture into the cavity of the duck and close with skewers or a trussing needle and thread.

Combine the skin coating ingredients until they are well blended. Place in a small saucepan and heat gently until the honey has dissolved.

Scald the skin of the duck with a kettleful of boiling water, turning the duck over once. Pat dry with kitchen paper towels. Hang the duck up by the neck in an airy place to dry for 1 hour. Brush the duck with the coating mixture and rehang to dry overnight.

Place the duck on a rack in a roasting pan and place in preheated hot oven, 220°C/425°F, Gas Mark 7. Roast for 10 minutes. Turn the duck over and roast for another 10 minutes. Reduce the temperature to moderately hot, 200°C/400°F, Gas Mark 6. Brush again with the coating mixture and roast for a final 10 minutes.

To serve, chop the duck into bite-size pieces and place on a warmed serving dish. Serve with the juices as gravy. SERVES 4 to 6.

CRISP DUCK WITH FIVE SPICES

METRIC/IMPERIAL	AMERICAN
1 × 2 kg/4½ lb duck	1 × 4½ lb duck
900 ml/1½ pints water	3¾ cups water
2 tablespoons soy sauce*	2 tablespoons soy sauce*
2 cloves star anise*	2 cloves star anise*
1 teaspoon salt	1 teaspoon salt
1 tablespoon brown sugar	1 tablespoon brown sugar
2 teaspoons five spice powder*	2 teaspoons five spice powder*
1 tablespoon salted black beans*	1 tablespoon salted black beans*
1 tablespoon medium or dry sherry	1 tablespoon cream or pale dry sherry
1 tablespoon cornflour	1 tablespoon cornstarch
1 tablespoon plain flour	1 tablespoon all-purpose flour
peanut oil for deep-frying	peanut oil for deep-frying
fruit chutney, to serve	fruit chutney, to serve

Place the duck in a large saucepan with the water, soy sauce, star anise, salt and brown sugar. Bring to the boil and simmer for 2 hours or until tender. Drain the duck well and dry with kitchen paper towels. Mix the five spice powder with the beans and the sherry and mash thoroughly. Place 1 teaspoon of the mixture inside the duck and rub the remainder over the outside. Sift the flours together and pat onto the outside of the duck.

Heat the oil in a deep-fryer to 180°C/350°F and deep-fry the duck until crisp and golden. Drain well on kitchen paper towels. Chop the duck through the bones into 8 eight pieces and serve hot with a fruit chutney. SERVES 8.

DUCK WITH ALMONDS

METRIC/IMPERIAL	AMERICAN
2 slices root ginger, peeled and shredded*	2 slices ginger root, peeled and shredded*
1 teaspoon salt	1 teaspoon salt
450 g/1 lb duck meat, cut into bite-size pieces	1 lb duck meat, cut into bite-size pieces
3 tablespoons vegetable oil	3 tablespoons vegetable oil
2 tablespoons cornflour	2 tablespoons cornstarch
3 tablespoons stock	3 tablespoons stock
2 tablespoons medium or dry sherry	2 tablespoons cream or pale dry sherry
2 spring onions, cut into 1 cm/ ½ inch lengths	2 scallions, cut into ½ inch lengths
1 teaspoon sugar	1 teaspoon sugar
2½ tablespoons soy sauce*	2½ tablespoons soy sauce*
5 tablespoons green peas	5 tablespoons green peas
5 tablespoons toasted almonds	5 tablespoons toasted almonds

Mix together the ginger and salt and rub into the duck with 1 tablespoon oil. Leave for 30 minutes. Combine the cornflour (cornstarch), stock and sherry until well blended.

Heat the remaining oil in a frying pan (skillet) over a high heat. Add the duck and spring onions (scallions) and stir-fry for 1½ minutes. Add the sugar and soy sauce and stir-fry for 30 seconds. Add the peas and almonds, then stir-fry for 1 minute. Add the cornflour (cornstarch) mixture and stir until the sauce thickens. Simmer for a final 30 seconds. Transfer to a warmed serving dish. SERVES 4.

Cantonese Roast Duck

Pork

BEAN SPROUTS WITH SHREDDED PORK

METRIC/IMPERIAL	AMERICAN
350 g/12 oz boned lean pork, shredded	1½ cups shredded pork loin
2 tablespoons soy sauce*	2 tablespoons soy sauce*
1 teaspoon medium or dry sherry	1 teaspoon cream or pale dry sherry
2 teaspoons cornflour	2 teaspoons cornstarch
3 tablespoons vegetable oil	3 tablespoons vegetable oil
2 spring onions, shredded	2 scallions, shredded
1 slice root ginger, peeled and shredded*	1 slice ginger root, peeled and shredded*
1 teaspoon salt	1 teaspoon salt
225 g/8 oz fresh bean sprouts*	½ lb bean sprouts*
50 g/2 oz leeks, shredded	½ cup shredded leeks

Place the pork in a bowl and sprinkle with the soy sauce, sherry and cornflour (cornstarch). Mix well, then leave to marinate for 20 minutes.

Heat 1 tablespoon of the oil in a wok or frying pan (skillet). Add the spring onions (scallions) and ginger, then the pork. Stir-fry until the pork changes colour, then remove the pork from the pan with a slotted spoon and drain.

Heat the remaining oil in the pan. Add the salt, then the bean sprouts and leeks. Stir-fry for about 1 minute. Return the pork to the pan, stir well and cook for a further minute. Transfer to a warmed serving dish and serve immediately. SERVES 4.

RED-COOKED PORK WITH MUSHROOMS

METRIC/IMPERIAL	AMERICAN
4 Chinese dried mushrooms, soaked in warm water for 30 minutes*	4 Chinese dried mushrooms, soaked in warm water for 30 minutes*
1 × 1.5 kg/3–3½ lb leg or shoulder of pork	1 × 3–3½ lb leg or shoulder of pork
1 garlic clove, crushed	1 garlic clove, crushed
6 tablespoons soy sauce*	6 tablespoons soy sauce*
3 tablespoons medium or dry sherry	3 tablespoons cream or pale dry sherry
3 tablespoons crystallized or brown sugar	3 tablespoons rock or brown sugar
1 teaspoon five spice powder*	1 teaspoon five spice powder*
To garnish:	For garnish:
1 carrot, thinly sliced into rounds	1 carrot, thinly sliced into rounds
shredded spring onion	shredded scallion

Drain the mushrooms, squeeze dry and discard the stems. Place the pork in a large pan and cover with cold water. Bring to the boil, boil for a few minutes then drain. Rinse the pork under cold running water, then drain again.

Return the pork to the cleaned pan. Add the mushrooms, garlic, soy sauce, sherry, sugar and five spice powder. Cover with a tight-fitting lid and bring to the boil. Lower the heat and simmer gently for 2 to 3 hours, turning the pork several times during the cooking. There should be very liquid left at the end of the cooking time. If necessary, increase the heat and simmer, covered, until the liquid has reduced and thickened. Serve hot or cold, garnished with carrot slices and shredded spring onion (scallion). SERVES 6 to 8.

PORK SLICES WITH CAULIFLOWER

METRIC/IMPERIAL	AMERICAN
4 Chinese dried mushrooms, soaked in warm water for 30 minutes*	4 Chinese dried mushrooms, soaked in warm water for 30 minutes*
225 g/8 oz boned lean pork, sliced	½ lb pork loin, sliced
2 tablespoons soy sauce*	2 tablespoons soy sauce*
1 tablespoon medium or dry sherry	1 tablespoon cream or pale dry sherry
1 tablespoon cornflour	1 tablespoon cornstarch
1 medium cauliflower, divided into florets	1 medium cauliflower, divided into florets
	salt

**Red-Cooked Pork; Pork Slices with Cauliflower; Bean Sprouts
with Shredded Pork**

salt
3 tablespoons vegetable oil
*2 spring onions, cut into 2.5
  cm/1 inch lengths*
*1 slice root ginger, peeled and
  cut into strips**

3 tablespoons vegetable oil
*2 scallions, cut into 1 inch
  lengths*
*1 slice ginger root, peeled and
  cut into strips**

Drain the mushrooms, squeeze dry and discard the stems.
Cut the caps into halves or quarters, according to size. Place
the pork in a bowl and sprinkle with the soy sauce, sherry,
and 1 teaspoon of the cornflour. Mix well, then leave to
marinate for 20 minutes.

Blanch the cauliflower in boiling, salted water for 1 to 2
minutes, then drain and reserve.

Heat the oil in a large wok or frying pan (skillet). Add the
spring onions (scallions) and ginger, then the pork. Stir-fry
until the pork changes colour, then add the mushrooms and
1 teaspoon salt. Stir-fry for another minute then add the
cauliflower and stir well. Mix the remaining cornflour to a
paste with a little water, add to the pan and stir constantly
until the mixture has thickened.

Arrange the cauliflower around the edge of a warmed
serving dish and pile the pork mixture into the centre.
SERVES 4.

43

ANTS CLIMBING TREES

METRIC/IMPERIAL

225 g/8 oz boned pork, minced
2 tablespoons soy sauce*
1 tablespoon sugar
1 teaspoon cornflour
½ teaspoon chilli sauce
3 tablespoons vegetable oil
1 small red chilli, chopped
2 spring onions, chopped
75 g/3 oz transparent noodles,
    soaked in water for 30
    minutes
120 ml/4 fl oz chicken stock
    or water
shredded spring onion, to
    garnish

AMERICAN

1 cup ground pork
2 tablespoons soy sauce*
1 tablespoon sugar
1 teaspoon cornstarch
½ teaspoon chili sauce
3 tablespoons vegetable oil
1 small red chili, chopped
2 scallions, chopped
3 oz cellophane noodles, soaked
    in water for 30 minutes
½ cup chicken stock or water
shredded scallion, for garnish

Place the pork in a bowl with the soy sauce, sugar, cornflour (cornstarch) and chilli sauce. Mix well, then leave to marinate for 20 minutes.

Heat the oil in a wok or frying pan (skillet), add the chilli and spring onions (scallions) and stir-fry for a few seconds. Add the pork and stir-fry until it changes colour.

Drain the noodles and add to the pan. Blend well, then add the stock or water and continue cooking until all the liquid has been absorbed. Serve hot, garnished with shredded spring onion (scallion). SERVES 4.

Mu-Hsu Pork; Ants Climbing Trees

MU-HSU PORK

METRIC/IMPERIAL	AMERICAN
25 g/1 oz tiger lily*, soaked in warm water for 20 minutes	¾ cup lily flowers*, soaked in warm water for 20 minutes
15 g/½ oz wood ears*, soaked in warm water for 20 minutes	½ cup tree ears*, soaked in warm water for 20 minutes
4 eggs	4 eggs
salt	salt
3 tablespoons vegetable oil	3 tablespoons vegetable oil
4 spring onions, shredded	4 scallions, shredded
225 g/8 oz pork fillet, shredded	1 cup shredded pork loin
1 tablespoon soy sauce	1 tablespoon soy sauce
1 teaspoon medium or dry sherry	1 teaspoon medium or pale dry sherry
1 teaspoon sesame seed oil*	1 teaspoon sesame seed oil*

Drain the tiger lily (lily flowers) and wood (tree) ears, discard any hard bits and shred finely.

Beat the eggs with a little salt. Heat 1 tablespoon of the oil in a wok or frying pan (skillet). Add the eggs and scramble lightly, removing them from the pan before they set too hard.

Heat the remaining oil in the same pan. Add the spring onions (scallions) and pork and stir-fry until the pork changes colour. Add the tiger lily (lily flowers) and wood (tree) ears, 1 teaspoon salt, the soy sauce and sherry. Stir-fry for about 2 minutes, then add the scrambled eggs and sesame seed oil. Mix all the ingredients well together. Serve hot. SERVES 4.

QUICK-FRIED PORK IN SWEET AND SOUR SAUCE WITH PEPPERS AND TOMATOES

METRIC/IMPERIAL	AMERICAN
450 g/1 lb lean boned leg of pork, cut into cubes	1 lb lean boned leg of pork, cut into cubes
1 tablespoon flour	1 tablespoon flour
1 teaspoon salt	1 teaspoon salt
4 tablespoons vegetable oil	4 tablespoons vegetable oil
1 medium green pepper, cored, seeded and diced	1 medium green pepper, cored, seeded and diced
3 medium tomatoes, cut into quarters	3 medium tomatoes, cut into quarters
450 g/1 lb cooked rice	6 cups cooked rice
Sauce:	Sauce:
1¼ tablespoons sugar	1¼ tablespoons sugar
2 tablespoons white wine vinegar	2 tablespoons white wine vinegar
1 tablespoon tomato purée	1 tablespoon tomato paste
3 tablespoons orange juice	3 tablespoons orange juice
1 tablespoon soy sauce*	1 tablespoon soy sauce*
1 tablespoon cornflour	1 tablespoon cornstarch
4 tablespoons water	4 tablespoons water

Rub the pork cubes all over with the flour and sprinkle with salt. Combine all the sauce ingredients until well blended.

Heat the oil in a large frying pan (skillet) over high heat. When the oil is very hot, add the pork cubes. Stir-fry for 2½ minutes. Add the pepper and tomatoes and stir-fry for 1 minutes. Pour in the sauce and gently toss and turn until all the ingredients are well coated. Cook for a few seconds more, until the sauce thickens.

To serve, arrange the rice on a warmed serving dish and spoon the pork mixture into the centre. SERVES 6 to 8.

BARBECUED SPARE RIBS

METRIC/IMPERIAL	AMERICAN
1.5 kg/3½ lb pork spare ribs	3-3½ lb country-style ribs
3 tablespoons vegetable oil	3 tablespoons vegetable oil
5 tablespoons soy sauce*	5 tablespoons soy sauce*
5 tablespoons water	5 tablespoons water
2 tablespoons hoisin sauce*	2 tablespoons hoisin sauce*
1 teaspoon sugar	1 teaspoon sugar
3-4 slices root ginger, peeled and shredded*	3-4 slices ginger root, peeled and shredded*
2 medium onions, thinly sliced	2 medium onions, thinly sliced
5 tablespoons dry sherry	⅓ cup dry sherry
salt	salt
freshly ground black pepper	freshly ground black pepper
5 tablespoons clear stock	⅓ cup clear stock

Blanch the pork in boiling water for 2 minutes, then drain. Heat the oil in a flameproof casserole, add the pork and stir-fry for 5 minutes. Add the soy sauce, water, hoisin sauce, sugar, ginger and onions. Stir and turn until the ingredients are well blended.

Place the casserole in a preheated cool oven 150°C/300°F, Gas Mark 2 for 1 hour, stirring twice. At the first stirring, add the sherry and the salt and pepper.

Remove the pork ribs and place them side by side in a roasting pan. Place them in the oven and increase the temperature to hot, 230°C/450°F, Gas Mark 8. Roast for 12 to 15 minutes. Set the casserole over a moderate heat, add the stock and stir-fry for 2 to 3 minutes. Arrange the pork ribs on a warmed serving dish and pour the gravy over before serving. SERVES 4 to 6.

RED-COOKED PORK WITH SPRING ONIONS (SCALLIONS) AND EGGS

METRIC/IMPERIAL	AMERICAN
1½ teaspoons sugar	1½ teaspoons sugar
120 ml/4 fl oz water	½ cup water
250 ml/8 fl oz soy sauce*	1 cup soy sauce*
1.5-2 kg/3½-4½ lb belly of pork, cut into 3.5 cm/1½ inch pieces	3½-4½ lb fresh pork sides, cut into 1½ inch pieces
5 tablespoons dry sherry	5 tablespoons dry sherry
3½ tablespoons vegetable oil	3½ tablespoons vegetable oil
4-5 spring onions, cut into 2.5 cm/1 inch pieces	4-5 scallions, cut into 1 inch pieces
3 garlic cloves, crushed	3 garlic cloves, crushed
4 hard-boiled eggs	4 hard-cooked eggs

Mix the sugar, water and 5½ tablespoons of the soy sauce until well blended. Place the pork in a flameproof casserole and pour over enough boiling water to cover. Cook for 15 minutes, then drain off all the water. Pour in the soy sauce mixture. Stir and turn the pork pieces in the sauce until they are well coated.

Place the casserole in a preheated cool oven, 150°C/300°F, Gas Mark 2 for 1 hour, stirring twice. Stir in

the sherry and cook for a further 1 hour, stirring twice.

Heat the vegetable oil in a frying pan (skillet) and stir-fry the spring onions (scallions) and garlic for 3 minutes. Pour the remaining soy sauce into a pan with the eggs and simmer for 7 to 8 minutes, or until brown.

To serve, spoon the spring onions (scallions) onto a warmed serving dish, pour the pork mixture on top and surround with the eggs. SERVES 4 to 6.

RED-COOKED PORK WITH CHESTNUTS

METRIC/IMPERIAL	AMERICAN
1½ teaspoons sugar	1½ teaspoons sugar
120 ml/4 fl oz water	½ cup water
5½ tablespoons soy sauce*	5½ tablespoons soy sauce*
1.5-2 kg/3½-4½ lb belly of pork, cut into 3.5 cm/1½ inch pieces	3½-4½ lb fresh pork sides, cut into 1½ inch pieces
225 g/8 oz peeled chestnuts	3 cups peeled chestnuts
5 tablespoons dry sherry	5 tablespoons dry sherry

Mix together the sugar, water and soy sauce until well blended. Place the pork in a flameproof casserole and pour over enough boiling water to cover. Cook for 15 minutes, then drain off all the water. Pour in the soy sauce mixture. Heat, stirring the pork pieces in the sauce until they are well coated. Place the casserole in a preheated cool oven, 150°C/300°F, Gas Mark 2 for 1 hour, stirring twice.

Cook the chestnuts in boiling water for 30 minutes, then drain. Add to the casserole with the sherry and mix well. Return to the oven for 1 hour, stirring twice. SERVES 4 to 6.

RED ROAST PORK

METRIC/IMPERIAL	AMERICAN
450 g/1 lb pork fillet	1 lb pork tenderloin
1 tablespoon hoisin sauce*	1 tablespoon hoisin sauce*
1 teaspoon five spice powder*	1 teaspoon five spice powder*
1 tablespoon soy sauce	1 tablespoon soy sauce*
½ tablespoon soft brown sugar	½ tablespoon firmly packed light brown sugar
1 garlic clove, crushed	1 garlic clove, crushed
1 teaspoon finely chopped root ginger*	1 teaspoon finely chopped ginger root*
peanut oil	peanut oil

Trim the pork but leave in 1 piece. Mix all the remaining ingredients except the oil and combine them thoroughly. Place the meat in a dish, brush with the oil and coat in the sauce. Leave to marinate for 1 to 20 hours.

Spoon more oil over the pork, place on a rack in a roasting pan and place in a preheated hot oven, 220°C/425°F, Gas Mark 7 for 10 minutes. Reduce the temperature to moderate, 180°C/350°F, Gas Mark 4 and roast for 30 to 35 minutes. Cut the meat diagonally and serve on a hot serving dish. SERVES 4.

Barbecued Spare Ribs

STIR-FRIED PORK WITH MUSHROOMS

METRIC/IMPERIAL	AMERICAN
450 g/1 lb lean pork, cut into 4 × 2.5 cm/1 inch slices	1 lb lean pork, cut into 4 × 1 inch slices
2 tablespoons soy sauce*	2 tablespoons soy sauce*
1½ tablespoons hoisin sauce*	1½ tablespoons hoisin sauce*
3½ tablespoons vegetable oil	3½ tablespoons vegetable oil
1 tablespoon sherry	1 tablespoon sherry
1 teaspoon sugar	1 teaspoon sugar
1½ tablespoons tomato purée	1½ tablespoons tomato paste
1 teaspoon chilli sauce	1 teaspoon chili sauce
1½ tablespoons butter	1½ tablespoons butter
6–8 medium mushrooms, stems and caps cut into quarters	6–8 medium mushrooms, stems and caps cut into quarters
1½ teaspoons cornflour	1½ teaspoons cornstarch
3 tablespoons water	3 tablespoons water

Stir-Fried Pork with Mushrooms; Pork and Bean Curd

Rub the pork slices with half of each of the next seven ingredients. Leave for 30 minutes.

Heat the butter in a small saucepan. Add the mushroom stems and stir-fry for 2 minutes. Add the mushroom caps and stir-fry for 1 minute.

Heat the remaining oil in a large frying pan (skillet) over a high heat. Add the pork and marinade and stir-fry for 2 minutes. Add the mushrooms and the remaining soy sauce, hoisin sauce, sugar, tomato purée (paste), sherry and chilli sauce. Stir-fry for 1½ minutes. Blend the cornflour (cornstarch) with the water and add to the pan. Heat stirring until the sauce thickens. Transfer the pork and sauce to a warmed serving dish. SERVES 4.

PORK AND BEAN CURD

METRIC/IMPERIAL	AMERICAN
1 kg/2 lb lean pork, cut into cubes	2 lb lean pork, cut into cubes
900 ml/1½ pints water	3¾ cups water
4 tablespoons soy sauce*	¼ cup soy sauce*
1 tablespoon medium or dry sherry	1 tablespoon cream or pale dry sherry
1 teaspoon brown sugar	1 teaspoon brown sugar
1 teaspoon salt	1 teaspoon salt
2 tablespoons vegetable oil	2 tablespoons vegetable oil
225 g/8 oz bean curd, cut into 5 cm/2 inch squares*	½ lb bean curd, cut into 2 inch squares*
1 spring onion, chopped	1 scallion, chopped

Place the pork cubes into a saucepan with 600 ml/1 pint (2½ cups) water. Bring to the boil, skim off the scum, cover the pan and simmer for 1 hour. Add 2 tablespoons of soy sauce, the sherry, sugar and salt. Cover and cook for another 30 minutes. Heat the oil in a frying an (skillet) and fry the bean curd for 2 to 3 minutes, turning it once during cooking. Add the remaining soy sauce, remaining water and the spring onion (scallion). Stir well and cook for 10 minutes, stirring occasionally. Mix the bean curd mixture into the pork and pour into a warmed serving dish. SERVES 6–8.

STIR-FRIED KIDNEY FLOWERS

METRIC/IMPERIAL	AMERICAN
15 g/½ oz wood ears, soaked in warm water for 30 minutes*	½ cup tree ears, soaked in warm water for 30 minutes*
225 g/8 oz pigs' kidneys	½ lb pork kidney
1½ teaspoons salt	1½ teaspoons salt
2 teaspoons cornflour	2 teaspoons cornstarch
6 tablespoons vegetable oil	6 tablespoons vegetable oil
1 garlic clove, crushed	1 garlic clove, crushed
1 slice root ginger, peeled and finely chopped*	1 slice ginger root, peeled and finely chopped*
1 spring onion, finely chopped	1 scallion, finely chopped
50 g/2 oz water chestnuts, sliced*	½ cup sliced water chestnuts*
50 g/2 oz bamboo shoots, sliced*	½ cup sliced bamboo shoots*
100 g/4 oz seasonal green vegetables (lettuce, cabbage or spinach), blanched in boiling water and drained	¼ lb seasonal green vegetables (lettuce, cabbage or spinach), blanched in boiling water and drained
1 tablespoon vinegar	1 tablespoon vinegar
1 tablespoon soy sauce*	1 tablespoon soy sauce*

Drain the wood (tree) ears and discard the hard bits. Split the kidneys in half lengthwise and discard the fat and white core. Score the surface in a criss-cross pattern then cut into pieces. Sprinkle with ½ teaspoon salt and 1 teaspoon cornflour (cornstarch).

Heat the oil in a frying pan (skillet) until it reaches smoking point. Add the kidneys and stir-fry until evenly browned. Remove from the pan with a slotted spoon and drain. Pour off all but 2 tablespoons of oil, then add the garlic, ginger and spring onion (scallion) to the pan. Stir-fry for a few seconds then add the wood (tree) ears, water chestnuts, bamboo shoots and green vegetables.

Stir in the vinegar and remaining salt, then return the kidneys to the pan. Mix the remaining cornflour (cornstarch) to a paste with a little water and add to the pan with the soy sauce. Cook, stirring, for 1 minute. Transfer the kidneys and vegetables to a warmed serving dish. SERVES 4.

LION'S HEAD MEATBALLS

METRIC/IMPERIAL	AMERICAN
450 g/1 lb minced pork	2 cups ground pork
225 g/8 oz belly of pork, shredded	½ lb fresh pork sides, shredded
1 medium onion, thinly sliced	1 medium onion, thinly sliced
2 garlic cloves, shredded	2 garlic cloves, shredded
4 medium water chestnuts, finely chopped*	4 medium water chestnuts, finely chopped*
4 tablespoons soy sauce*	4 tablespoons soy sauce*
1 teaspoon salt	1 teaspoon salt
1½ tablespoons water	1½ tablespoons water
1 tablespoon cornflour	1 tablespoon cornstarch
2½ tablespoons vegetable oil	2½ tablespoons vegetable oil
150 ml/¼ pint clear stock	⅔ cup clear stock
2 tablespoons dry sherry	2 tablespoons dry sherry
100 g/4 oz transparent noodles, soaked in hot water for 5 minutes	¼ cellophane noodles, soaked in hot water for 5 minutes

Mix the minced (ground) pork with the shredded pork, onion, garlic, water chestnuts, 2 tablespoons soy sauce, salt, water and cornflour (cornstarch). Beat until well blended them form the mixture into 4 equal-sized balls.

Heat the oil in a flameproof casserole. Add the meatballs and stir and turn them in the oil. Cook over a low heat for 7 to 8 minutes, until the meatballs are golden. Cover the casserole and place in a preheated cool oven 150°C/300°F, Gas Mark 2 for 2 hours, stirring gently every 30 minutes.

Remove the meatballs from the casserole and keep hot. Add the stock, sherry and remaining soy sauce to the casserole. Heat, stirring until the mixture boils, then add the noddles. Cook gently for 8 minutes until the noodles have absorbed most or all of the liquid.

To serve, spoon half the noodles into a warmed bowl and spread out evenly. Arrange 3 meatballs in the centre of the bowl then place the last meatball on top of the others. Use the remaining noodles to drape the 'lion's head'. SERVES 4.

CHA SHAO QUICK-ROAST PORK WITH CABBAGE

METRIC/IMPERIAL	AMERICAN
750 g/1½ lb pork fillet	1½ lb pork tenderloin
1 tablespoon butter	1 tablespoon butter
1 small cabbage, shredded	1 small cabbage, shredded
½ chicken stock cube	1 chicken bouillon cube
1 tablespoon soy sauce*	1 tablespoon soy sauce*
salt	salt
freshly ground black pepper	freshly ground black pepper
5–6 tablespoons water	5–6 tablespoons water
450 g/1 lb hot cooked rice	6 cups hot cooked rice
Marinade:	Marinade:
1½ tablespoons soy sauce*	1½ tablespoons soy sauce*
1 tablespoon hoisin sauce or soy paste*	1 tablespoon hoisin sauce or soy paste*
1½ teaspoons soy jam*	1½ teaspoons soy jam*
½ teaspoon salt	½ teaspoon salt
1½ tablespoons vegetable oil	1½ tablespoons vegetable oil
1½ teaspoons sugar	1½ teaspoons sugar

Combine all the marinade ingredients until they are well blended. Add the pork and baste well. Leave for 2 to 2½ hours, turning the pork every 30 minutes.

Arrange the pork on a rack in a roasting pan. Place in a preheated hot oven 230°C/450°F, Gas Mark 8 for 12 to 14 minutes, turning once. Remove the pork from the oven and keep hot.

Place the roasting pan (with the drippings) over a moderate heat and add the butter. When the butter has melted, add the cabbage. Stir and turn to coat well. Sprinkle with the crumbled stock (bouillon) cube, soy sauce, pepper and water. Increase the heat to high, cover and cook for 2 to 3 minutes, adding more water if necessary.

To serve, cut the pork across the grain into thin slices. Arrange the cooked rice on a warmed serving dish and top with the pork, gravy and cabbage. SERVES 6 to 8.

DOUBLE-COOKED PORK

METRIC/IMPERIAL	AMERICAN
1½ tablespoons wood ears, soaked in warm water for 30 minutes*	1½ tablespoons tree ears, soaked in warm water for 30 minutes*
750 g/1½ lb belly pork	1½ lb fresh pork sides
3½ tablespoons vegetable oil	3½ tablespoons vegetable oil
2 dried chilli peppers, seeded and sliced, or 2 teaspoons chilli sauce	2 dried chili peppers, seeded and sliced, or 2 teaspoons chili sauce
4 garlic cloves, crushed	4 garlic cloves, crushed
1 tablespoon soy paste*	1 tablespoon soy paste*
2 tablespoons soy sauce*	2 tablespoons soy sauce*
1 tablespoon hoisin sauce, or sweet bean paste*	1 tablespoon hoisin sauce, or sweet bean paste*
2 tablespoons tomato purée	2 tablespoons tomato paste
2 teaspoons sugar	2 teaspoons sugar
3 tablespoons clear stock	3 tablespoons clear stock
4 spring onions, cut into 3.5 cm/1½ inch lengths	4 scallions, cut into 1½ inch lengths
1½ tablespoons medium or dry sherry	1½ tablespoons cream or pale dry sherry
1 tablespoon sesame seed oil*	1 tablespoon sesame seed oil*

Drain the wood (tree) ears, squeeze dry and discard the hard bits. Place the pork in a saucepan and cover with boiling water. Cover and simmer for 25 minutes. Leave to cool, then cut through the fat and skin into 3.5 cm/1½ inch slices.

Heat the oil in a frying pan (skillet) over moderate heat. When the oil is hot, add the chilli peppers and wood (tree) ears and stir-fry for 1 minute. Add the garlic, soy paste, soy sauce, hoisin sauce, tomato purée (paste), sugar and stock. Stir for 30 seconds, until the mixture becomes smooth. Add the pork slices and spread out in one layer. Increase the heat to high, stir and turn the pork in the sauce until it is well coated and the sauce begins to thicken. Sprinkle with spring onions (scallions), sherry and sesame oil, stir and turn a few more times. Transfer to a warmed serving dish. SERVES 4.

Lion's Head Meatballs

SWEET AND SOUR PORK WITH LYCHEES

Sweet and Sour Pork with Lychees; Crispy Pork

METRIC/IMPERIAL	AMERICAN
4 tablespoons soy sauce*	$\frac{1}{4}$ cup soy sauce*
1 tablespoon dry sherry	1 tablespoon dry sherry
1 teaspoon finely chopped root ginger*	1 teaspoon finely chopped ginger root*
pinch of monodosium glutamate*	pinch of monosodium glutamate*
450 g/1 lb shoulder of pork, cut into 2.5 cm/1 inch cubes	1 lb shoulder of pork, cut into 1 inch cubes
30 g/1¼ oz cornflour	5 tablespoons cornstarch
25 g/1 oz plain flour	$\frac{1}{4}$ cup all-purpose flour
salt	salt
2 eggs, beaten	2 eggs, beaten
oil for deep-frying	oil for deep-frying
$\frac{1}{2}$ red pepper, cored, seeded and cut into wedges	$\frac{1}{2}$ red pepper, cored, seeded and cut into wedges
$\frac{1}{2}$ green pepper, cored, seeded and cut into wedges	$\frac{1}{2}$ green pepper, cored, seeded and cut into wedges
2 apples, peeled, cored and quartered	2 apples, peeled, cored and quartered
1 tablespoon brown sugar	1 tablespoon brown sugar
150 ml/¼ pint syrup from canned lychees	$\frac{2}{3}$ cup syrup from canned lychees
2 tablespoons vinegar	2 tablespoons vinegar
4 spring onions, finely chopped	4 scallions, finely chopped
1 × 300 g/11 oz can lychees, drained	1 × 11 oz can lychees, drained

In a bowl mix together 3 tablespoons soy sauce, the sherry, ginger and monosodium glutamate. Add the pork, stir to coat and marinate for 1 to 2 hours.

Sift 25 g/1 oz (4 tablespoons) cornflour (cornstarch), the flour and a pinch of a salt into a bowl. Add the eggs gradually, beating well to make a smooth batter. Coat the pork cubes in the batter.

Heat the oil in a deep-fryer to 180°C/350°F and deep-fry the pork cubes until golden. Drain on kitchen paper towels and keep hot.

Mix the remaining ingredients in a small saucepan. Bring to the boil, stirring constantly, and simmer for 2 to 3 minutes. Place the pork on a heated serving dish and pour the sauce over. SERVES 4.

QUICK-FRIED PORK WITH BEAN SPROUTS AND SPRING ONIONS (SCALLIONS)

METRIC/IMPERIAL	AMERICAN
450 g/1 lb lean pork, cut into 2.5 cm/1 inch pieces	1 lb lean pork, cut into 1 inch pieces
2 tablespoons soy sauce*	2 tablespoons soy sauce*
4 tablespoons vegetable oil	4 tablespoons vegetable oil
1 teaspoon salt	1 teaspoon salt
1½ tablespoons butter	1½ tablespoons butter
350 g/12 oz bean sprouts*	$\frac{3}{4}$ lb bean sprouts*
4 spring onions, cut into 2.5 cm/1 inch lengths	4 scallions, cut into 1 inch lengths
1 teaspoon sugar	1 teaspoon sugar
2 tablespoons boiling water	2 tablespoons boiling water
1½ tablespoons dry sherry	1½ tablespoons dry sherry
450 g/1 lb hot cooked rice	6 cups hot cooked rice

Rub the pork pieces all over with 1 tablespoon soy sauce and 1 tablespoon oil. Sprinkle with salt.

Heat the remaining oil in a large frying pan (skillet) over

a high heat. When the oil is hot, add the pork. Stir-fry for 2¼ minutes, then remove from the pan.

Melt the butter in the pan and add the bean sprouts and spring onions (scallions). Stir-fry for 1 minute. Sprinkle with the remaining soy sauce, the sugar and water. Stir-fry for 30 seconds. Return the pork to the pan. Add the sherry and stir-fry for 1 minute. Arrange the cooked rice on a warmed serving dish and spoon the pork mixture into the centre. SERVES 4.

CRISPY PORK

METRIC/IMPERIAL	AMERICAN
450 g/1 lb lean pork, cut into 2.5 cm/1 inch cubes	1 lb lean pork, cut into 1 inch cubes
600 ml/1 pint water	2½ cups water
2 tablespoons soy sauce*	2 tablespoons soy sauce*
1 tablespoon sugar	1 tablespoon sugar
1 clove star anis*	1 clove star anise*
1 tablespoon medium or dry sherry (optional)	1 tablespoon cream or pale dry sherry (optional)
pinch of monosodium glutamate*	pinch of monosodium glutamate*
100 g/4 oz self-raising flour	1 cup self-raising flour
pinch of salt	pinch of salt
1 egg	1 egg
vegetable oil for frying	vegetable oil for frying

Place the pork cubes in a saucepan with 450 ml/¾ pint (2 cups) water, the soy sauce, sugar, star anise, sherry and monosodium glutamate. Bring to the boil, cover and simmer for 45 minutes or until tender. Drain well.

Sift the flour and salt into a bowl. Make a well in the centre, add the egg and mix with a wooden spoon, gradually bringing in the flour from the edge. Add the remaining water gradually, beating continually. Add the pork pieces and stir to coat in the batter.

Heat the oil in a frying pan (skillet) or deep-fryer to 180°C/350°F and deep-fry the pork pieces until crisp and golden. Drain well on kitchen paper towels. Serve in a warmed dish. SERVES 4.

PORK WITH MUSHROOMS AND CAULIFLOWER

METRIC/IMPERIAL	AMERICAN
1 kg/2 lb pork chops	2 lb center cut pork chops
600 ml/1 pint water	2½ cups water
100 g/4 oz Chinese dried mushrooms, soaked in warm water for 30 minutes*	¼ lb Chinese dried mushrooms, soaked in warm water for 30 minutes*
4 tablespoons soy sauce*	¼ cup soy sauce*
3 tablespoons medium or dry sherry	3 tablespoons cream or pale dry sherry
4 spring onions	4 scallions
1 teaspoon brown sugar	1 teaspoon brown sugar
1 teaspoon salt	1 teaspoon salt
1 cauliflower, divided into florets	1 cauliflower, divided into florets

Wipe the chops, place them in a large pan and cover with the water. Bring to the boil, skim off the scum, cover the pan with a tight-fitting lid and simmer for 30 minutes.

Drain the mushrooms, squeeze dry, discard the stems and chop finely. Add to the pan with the soy sauce, sherry, spring onions (scallions), sugar and salt. Cover and simmer for a further 45 minutes. Add the cauliflower to the pan, mix well and cook for a further 15 minutes. Arrange the chops and vegetables on a warmed serving dish. SERVES 6.

Beef

STIR-FRIED BEEF WITH CELERY AND CABBAGE

METRIC/IMPERIAL	AMERICAN
450 g/1 lb rump steak, cut into 2.5 cm/1 inch slices	1 lb top round steak, cut into 1 inch slices
2 slices root ginger, peeled and shredded*	2 slices ginger root, peeled and shredded*
1 teaspoon sugar	1 teaspoon sugar
3 tablespoons soy sauce*	3 tablespoons soy sauce*
4 tablespoons vegetable oil	4 tablespoons vegetable oil
2 teaspoons cornflour	2 teaspoons cornstarch
2 tablespoons stock or water	2 tablespoons stock or broth or water
2 tablespoons medium or dry sherry	2 tablespoons cream or pale dry sherry
2 celery sticks, cut into 2.5 cm/1 inch lengths	2 stalks celery, cut into 1 inch lengths
100–150 g/4–5 oz white or Chinese cabbage, roughly chopped	1½–2 cups shredded white cabbage or bok choy

Quick-Fried Beef with Sweet Peppers in Black Bean Sauce; Stir-Fried Beef with Celery and Cabbage

Rub the meat slices with the ginger, sugar, 2 tablespoons of the soy sauce and 1 tablespoon of oil. Leave for 10 minutes. Combine the cornflour (cornstarch), stock and sherry until they are well blended.

Heat the remaining oil in a large frying pan (skillet) over high heat. When the oil is very hot, add the beef, celery and cabbage. Stir-fry for 2½ minutes. Sprinkle with the remaining soy sauce and the cornflour (cornstarch) mixture and stir-fry for 1 minute, or until the sauce thickens. Transfer to a hot serving dish. SERVES 4.

QUICK-FRIED BEEF WITH SWEET PEPPERS IN BLACK BEAN SAUCE

METRIC/IMPERIAL	AMERICAN
550–750 g/1¼–1½ lb beef steak, cut into 4 x 2.5 cm/1 inch slices	1¼–1½ lb beef steak, cut into 4 x 1 inch slices
1 tablespoon soy sauce*	1 tablespoon soy sauce*
1 tablespoon soy paste*	1 tablespoon soy paste*
1 tablespoon hoisin sauce (optional)*	1 tablespoon hoisin sauce (optional)*
1 tablespoon tomato purée	1 tablespoon tomato paste
1½ tablespoons cornflour	1½ tablespoons cornstarch
4½ tablespoons vegetable oil	4½ tablespoons vegetable oil
1¼ teaspoons sugar	1½ teaspoons sugar
2 teaspoons salted black beans, soaked*	2 teaspoons salted black beans, soaked*
2–3 slices root ginger, peeled and shredded*	2–3 slices ginger root, peeled and shredded*
1 medium red pepper, cored, seeded and cut into 4 x 1 cm/½ inch pieces	1 medium red pepper, cut into 4 x ½ inch pieces
1 medium green pepper, cored, seeded and cut into 4 x 1 cm/½ inch pieces	1 medium green pepper, cut into 4 x ½ inch pieces
3 tablespoons dry sherry	3 tablespoons dry sherry

Rub the meat slices all over with the soy sauce, soy paste, hoisin sauce, tomato purée (paste), cornflour (cornstarch), 1 tablespoon oil and the sugar. Leave for 15 minutes.

Heat the remaining oil in a frying pan (skillet) over a high heat. When the oil is hot, add the black beans and ginger. Stir-fry for 30 seconds. Add the beef and stir-fry for 2 minutes. Add the peppers and sprinkle with the sherry. Stir-fry for a further 1 minute. Transfer to a hot serving dish. SERVES 4.

SMOKED MEATBALLS

METRIC/IMPERIAL	AMERICAN
4 Chinese dried mushrooms, soaked in warm water for 30 minutes*	4 Chinese dried mushrooms, soaked in warm water for 30 minutes*
1 small can water chestnuts, drained, rinsed and finely chopped*	1 small can water chestnuts, drained, rinsed and finely chopped*
450 g/1 lb lean minced beef	1 lb ground beef
2 tablespoons soy sauce*	2 tablespoons soy sauce*
2 tablespoons cornflour	2 tablespoons cornstarch
1 tablespoon finely chopped spring onions	1 tablespoon finely chopped scallion
1 tablespoon finely chopped root ginger*	1 tablespoon finely chopped ginger root*
1 medium carrot, grated	1 medium carrot, grated
1 tablespoon Chinese rice wine or dry sherry	1 tablespoon Chinese rice wine or dry sherry
1 teaspoon sesame seed oil*	1 teaspoon sesame seed oil*
For smoking:	For smoking:
2 tablespoons brown sugar	2 tablespoons brown sugar
2 tablespoons black tea leaves	2 tablespoons black tea leaves
2 tablespoons fennel seeds	2 tablespoons fennel seeds
To serve:	To serve:
2 teaspoons sesame seed oil mixed with 2 tablespoons soy sauce*	2 teaspoons sesame seed oil mixed with 2 tablespoons soy sauce*
2 spring onions, finely chopped	2 scallions, finely chopped

Drain the mushrooms, squeeze dry, discard the stems and chop the caps finely. Place the mushrooms and chestnuts in a large bowl, add the remaining ingredients and mix well by hand until the mixture if firm and compact. Shape into walnut-sized balls and arrange in 1 layer on a greased wire rack or Chinese bamboo steamer. Cover and steam over boiling water in a wok or deep frying pan (skillet) for 15 minutes.

To smoke the meatballs, use an old frying pan (skillet), wok or other metal container lined with foil. Combine the brown sugar, tea leaves and fennel seeds and place in the bottom of the pan. Set over a high heat. When the mixture begins to smoke, put the rack containing the meatballs over the smoke. Cover tightly with a lid or foil and leave for 5 minutes. Turn the heat off and leave the meatballs, still covered, for another 10 minutes. Arrange on a hot serving dish and serve with the sesame seed and soy sauce mixture and spring onions (scallions). SERVES 4.

MANGE-TOUT PEAS AND BEEF

METRIC/IMPERIAL	AMERICAN
225 g/8 oz beef steak, thinly sliced	1 cup thinly sliced flank or round steak
2 tablespoons oyster sauce*	2 tablespoons oyster sauce*
1 tablespoon medium or dry sherry	1 tablespoon cream or pale dry sherry
1 teaspoon cornflour	1 teaspoon cornstarch
4 tablespoons vegetable oil	¼ cup vegetable oil
2 spring onions, cut into 2.5 cm/1 inch lengths	2 scallions, cut into 1 inch lengths
1 slice root ginger, peeled and cut into strips*	1 slice ginger root, peeled and cut into strips*
225 g/8 oz mange-tout, topped and tailed	½ lb snow peas, topped and tailed
1 tablespoon salt	1 tablespoon salt
1 teaspoon sugar	1 teaspoon sugar

Place the beef in a bowl with the oyster sauce, sherry and cornflour (cornstarch). Mix well, then leave to marinate for 20 minutes.

Heat 2 tablespoons of oil in a wok or frying pan (skillet). Add the spring onions (scallions) and ginger. Stir-fry for a few seconds then add the meat. Stir-fry until evenly browned, then transfer to a serving dish and keep hot.

Heat the remaining oil in the pan. Add the mange-tout (snow peas), salt and sugar and stir-fry for 2 minutes. Do not over-cook or the mange-tout (snow peas) will lose their texture and colour. Add them to the meat and mix well. Serve immediately. SERVES 4.

STIR-FRIED BEEF WITH BROCCOLI

METRIC/IMPERIAL	AMERICAN
225 g/8 oz beef steak, thinly sliced	½ lb flank or round steak, thinly sliced
2 teaspoons salt	2 teaspoons salt
1 teaspoon medium or dry sherry	1 teaspoon cream or pale dry sherry
1 tablespoon cornflour	1 tablespoon cornstarch
4 tablespoons vegetable oil	¼ cup vegetable oil
225 g/8 oz broccoli, divided into florets	½ lb broccoli, divided into florets
a little chicken stock or water (optional)	a little chicken stock or water (optional)
2 spring onions, cut into 2.5 cm/1 inch lengths	2 scallions, cut into 1 inch lengths
100 g/4 oz button mushrooms, sliced	1 cup sliced button mushrooms
1 tablespoon soy sauce*	1 tablespoon soy sauce*

Beef and Carrot Stew; Stir-Fried Beef with Broccoli; Mange-Tout Peas and Beef

Place the sliced steak in a bowl with 1 teaspoon salt, the sherry and cornflour (cornstarch). Mix together well and leave for 20 minutes.

Heat 2 tablespoons of the oil in a wok or frying pan (skillet). Add the broccoli and remaining salt and stir-fry for a few minutes, adding a little stock or water to moisten if necessary. Remove from the pan with a slotted spoon and drain.

Heat the remaining oil in the pan. Add the spring onions (scallions) and stir-fry for a few seconds. Add the meat and stir-fry until evenly browned. Stir in the mushrooms, soy sauce and broccoli. Transfer to a hot serving dish and serve immediately. SERVES 4.

BEEF AND CARROT STEW

METRIC/IMPERIAL	AMERICAN
2 tablespoons vegetable oil	2 tablespoons vegetable oil
1 garlic clove, crushed	1 garlic clove, crushed
1 slice root ginger, peeled and chopped*	1 slice ginger root, peeled and chopped*
1 spring onion, chopped	1 scallion, chopped
750 g/1½ lb stewing beef, cut into 1 cm/½ inch squares	1½ lb beef chuck steak, cut into ½ inch squares
4 tablespoons soy sauce*	¼ cup soy sauce*
1 tablespoon sugar	1 tablespoon sugar
1 tablespoon sherry	1 tablespoon sherry
½ teaspoon five spice powder*	½ teaspoon five spice powder*
450 g/1 lb carrots, peeled and cut into diamond shapes	1 lb carrots, peeled and cut into diamond shapes

Heat the oil in a heavy pan or flameproof casserole. Add the garlic, ginger and spring onion (scallion) and fry until golden brown. Add the beef and the remaining ingredients except the carrots.

Add just enough cold water to cover. Bring to the boil, cover and simmer for 1½ hours. Add the carrots to the beef and simmer for 30 minutes or until the beef and carrots are tender. Transfer to a hot serving dish. SERVES 4

RED-COOKED BEEF

METRIC/IMPERIAL	AMERICAN
750 g/1½ lb stewing beef, in one piece	1½ lb beef chuck steak, in one piece
4 slices root ginger, peeled*	4 slices ginger root, peeled*
2 tablespoons medium or dry sherry	2 tablespoons cream or pale dry sherry
2 tablespoons vegetable oil	2 tablespoons vegetable oil
5 tablespoons soy sauce*	⅓ cup soy sauce*
1 tablespoon sugar	1 tablespoon sugar
1 tablespoon sesame seed oil (optional)*	1 tablespoon sesame seed oil (optional)*

Place the beef, ginger and sherry in a large pan. Add just enough water to cover and bring to the boil. Skim the surface, then lower the heat, cover and simmer gently for 1 hour.

Remove the beef from the pan, reserving the cooking liquid. Cut the beef into 2.5 cm/1 inch pieces

Heat the oil in a wok or frying pan (skillet), add the beef and stir-fry for 30 seconds, then add the soy sauce, sugar and reserved cooking liquid. Cover and simmer for 40 minutes, or until the beef is tender. Sprinkle with the sesame seed oil, if using. Serve hot. SERVES 4.

BEEF MEATBALLS WITH CABBAGE AND CELERY

METRIC/IMPERIAL	AMERICAN
2–3 water chestnuts, shredded (optional)*	2–3 water chestnuts, shredded (optional)*
350–450 g/¾–1 lb minced beef	¾–1 lb ground beef
½ teaspoon salt	½ teaspoon salt
1½ tablespoons soy sauce*	1½ tablespoons soy sauce*
1 tablespoon tomato purée	1 tablespoon tomato paste
2 tablespoons cornflour	2 tablespoons cornstarch
1 egg	1 egg
5 tablespoons vegetable oil	⅓ cup vegetable oil
1 medium cabbage, cut into 2.5 cm/1 inch slices	1 medium cabbage, cut into 1 inch slices
2 celery sticks, cut into 2.5 cm/1 inch lengths	2 stalks celery, cut into 1 inch lengths
½ chicken stock cube, dissolved in 150 ml/¼ pint hot stock	1 chicken bouillon cube, dissolved in ⅔ cup hot stock

Mix the chestnuts into the minced (ground) beef with the salt, soy sauce, tomato purée (paste), 1 tablespoon of cornflour (cornstarch) and the egg. Form the mixture into 10 to 12 meatballs. Dust the meatballs with the remaining cornflour (cornstarch) then coat with 1 tablespoon of oil.

Heat the remaining oil in a frying pan (skillet) over a moderate heat. When the oil is hot, add the meatballs. Cook for 7 to 8 minutes, until evenly browned. Remove from the pan and keep warm. Add the cabbage, celery and stock to the pan. Bring to the boil and cook, stirring continuously, for 2 or 3 minutes.

Transfer the cabbage, celery and stock to a casserole. Arrange the meatballs on top and cover. Place the casserole in a preheated moderately hot oven 190°C/375°F, Gas Mark 5 for 45 minutes. Serve hot. SERVES 6 to 8.

QUICK-FRIED BEEF WITH TOMATOES AND PEAS

METRIC/IMPERIAL	AMERICAN
450 g/1 lb fillet or rump of beef, cut into cubes	1 lb beef tenderloin or round steak, cut into cubes
4 tablespoons vegetable oil	4 tablespoons vegetable oil
1 teaspoon salt	1 teaspoon salt
freshly ground black pepper	freshly ground black pepper
2 tablespoons butter	2 tablespoons butter
2 medium onions, thinly sliced	2 medium onions, thinly sliced
2 spring onions, cut into 1 cm/½ inch lengths	2 scallions, cut into ½ inch lengths
225 g/8 oz shelled peas	1½ cup shelled peas
2–3 tomatoes, cut into quarters	2–3 tomatoes, cut into quarters
1 teaspoon sugar	1 teaspoon sugar
2 tablespoons soy sauce*	2 tablespoons soy sauce*
½ chicken stock cube	1 chicken bouillon cube
150 ml/¼ pint water	⅔ cup water
1 tablespoon cornflour	1 tablespoon cornstarch
450 g/1 lb cooked rice	6 cups cooked rice

Rub the meat all over with 1 tablespoon oil and sprinkle with salt and pepper. Heat the remaining oil and the butter in a large frying pan (skillet) over a high heat. When the fat has melted, add the onions and stir-fry for 1 minute. Add the spring onions (scallions), peas and tomatoes. Sprinkle with sugar, soy sauce, crumbled stock (bouillon) cube and 4 tablespoons water. Stir until the ingredients are well blended and bring to the boil.

Blend the cornflour (cornstarch) with the remaining water and add to the pan. Heat, stirring until the sauce thickens. To serve, arrange the cooked rice on a warmed serving dish and spoon the beef mixture into the centre. SERVES 4.

MASHED BEAN CURD WITH MINCED (GROUND) BEEF

METRIC/IMPERIAL	AMERICAN
4 tablespoons vegetable oil	4 tablespoons vegetable oil
2 teaspoons salted black beans, soaked*	2 teaspoons salted black beans, soaked*
5–6 medium Chinese dried mushrooms, soaked in 300 ml/½ pint warm water for 30 minutes*	5–6 medium Chinese dried mushrooms, soaked in 1¼ cups warm water for 30 minutes*
5–6 tablespoons minced beef	5–6 tablespoons ground beef
3 spring onions, cut into thin rounds	3 scallions, cut into thin rounds
4 garlic cloves, crushed	4 garlic cloves, crushed
2 tablespoons soy sauce*	2 tablespoons soy sauce*
2 tablespoons hoisin sauce*	2 tablespoons hoisin sauce*
2 teaspoons chilli sauce	2 teaspoons chili sauce
1 teaspoon sugar	1 teaspoon sugar
2–3 cakes bean curd*	2–3 cakes bean curd*
4 tablespoons clear stock	4 tablespoons clear stock
2 teaspoons cornflour	2 teaspoons cornstarch
3 tablespoons water	3 tablespoons water
1 tablespoon sesame seed oil*	1 tablespoon sesame seed oil*

Heat the oil in a large frying pan (skillet) over a moderate heat. When the oil is hot, add the black beans. Stir and turn in the oil for 15 seconds.

Drain the mushrooms, reserving the liquid, squeeze dry and cut into quarters, discarding the stems. Add to the pan with the meat and half the spring onions (scallions). Stir-fry for 3 to 4 minutes, until well blended. Add the garlic, 3–4 tablespoons of the mushroom liquid, the soy sauce, hoisin sauce, chilli sauce, sugar, bean curd and stock. Increase the heat to high and stir-fry the mixture until it comes to the boil. Simmer for 3 to 4 minutes. Blend the cornflour (cornstarch) with the water and add to the pan with the spring onions (scallions) and sesame seed oil. Stir and turn a few times more. Serve hot. SERVES 4.

BEEF IN CLEAR BROTH WITH TRANSPARENT NOODLES, CABBAGE, CHINESE MUSHROOMS AND SPRING ONIONS (SCALLIONS)

METRIC/IMPERIAL	AMERICAN
450 g/1 lb stewing steak, cut into cubes	1 lb beef chuck, cut into cubes
5–6 medium Chinese dried mushrooms, soaked in warm water for 30 minutes*	5–6 medium Chinese dried mushrooms, soaked in warm water for 30 minutes*
1 teaspoon salt	1 teaspoon salt
	½ teaspoon peppercorns

Beef Meatballs with Cabbage and Celery; Red-Cooked Beef

½ teaspoon peppercorns	3 tablespoons soy sauce*
3 tablespoons soy sauce*	2½ cups water
600 ml/1 pint water	4 oz cellophane noodles, soaked in hot water for 10 minutes
100 g/4 oz transparent noodles, soaked in hot water for 10 minutes	2 medium carrots, shredded
2 medium carrots, shredded	3 cups shredded cabbage or bok choy
225 g/8 oz cabbage or Chinese leaves, shredded	1¼ cups white wine
300 ml/½ pint white wine	2 chicken bouillon cubes
1 chicken stock cube	2–3 scallions, cut into ½ inch lengths
2–3 spring onions, cut into 2.5 cm/½ inch lengths	salt
salt	freshly ground black pepper
freshly ground black pepper	

Blanch the meat cubes in boiling water for 2 minutes and drain. Drain the mushrooms, squeeze dry, discard the stems and cut into quarters. Place the meat in a flameproof casserole. Add the salt, peppercorns, soy sauce and water and bring to the boil.

Place the casserole in a preheated moderate oven 180°C/350°F, Gas Mark 4 for 1 hour, stirring twice. Add the drained noodles, mushrooms and vegetables. Return to the oven and cook for 1 hour, stirring twice. Add the wine, crumbled stock cube (bouillon cubes) and cook for a further 50 minutes. Sprinkle with spring onions (scallions) and add salt and pepper to taste. Return to the oven for a final 10 minutes. Serve hot. SERVES 4.

Lamb

STIR-FRIED LAMB WITH NOODLES AND SPRING ONIONS (SCALLION)

METRIC/IMPERIAL	AMERICAN
1 egg	1 egg
1 tablespoon cornflour	1 tablespoon cornstarch
1½ tablespoons water	1½ tablespoons water
225 g/8 oz lean lamb, cut into thin strips	½ lb boneless lamb for stew, cut into strips
3 tablespoons vegetable oil	3 tablespoons vegetable oil
2 tablespoons soy sauce*	2 tablespoons soy sauce*
4-5 spring onions, cut into 5 cm/2 inch lengths	4-5 scallions, cut into 2 inch lengths
1 chicken stock cube, dissolved in 300 ml/½ pint stock	2 chicken bouillon cubes, dissolved in 1¼ cups stock
100 g/4 oz transparent noodles, soaked in hot water for 5 minutes	4 oz cellophane noodles, soaked in hot water for 5 minutes
1 tablespoon sesame seed oil*	1 tablespoon sesame seed oil*
2 tablespoons sherry	2 tablespoons sherry

Beat the egg lightly then blend with the cornflour (cornstarch) and water to make a batter. Add the lamb to the batter, and turn to coat the strips.

Heat the oil in a large frying pan (skillet) over a high heat.

Add the lamb strips and spread evenly over the pan. Stir-fry for 1 minute. Add the stock and drained noodles and bring to the boil, stirring. Reduce the heat, cover and simmer gently for 5 minutes. Sprinkle with sesame seed oil and sherry. Simmer for a further 1 minute. Transfer to a warmed serving dish. SERVES 4.

STIR-FRIED LAMBS' KIDNEYS WITH CELERY AND FRENCH (GREEN) BEANS

METRIC/IMPERIAL	AMERICAN
3-4 lambs' kidneys, skinned, cored and cut into strips	3-4 lambs' kidneys, skinned, cored and cut into strips
1 tablespoon soy paste or hoisin sauce*	1 tablespoon soy paste or hoisin sauce*
1½ tablespoons soy sauce*	1½ tablespoons soy sauce*
1 tablespoon vinegar	1 tablespoon vinegar
3 tablespoons vegetable oil	3 tablespoons vegetable oil
1 teaspoon sugar	1 teaspoon sugar
½ chicken stock cube, dissolved in 6 tablespoons clear stock	1 chicken bouillon cube, dissolved in 6 tablespoons clear stock
100 g/4 oz French beans, sliced	½ cup sliced green beans
2-3 celery sticks, chopped	2-3 stalks celery, chopped
1 tablespoon butter	1 tablespoon butter

Score each kidney strip with criss-cross cuts half-way through. Combine the soy paste, soy sauce, vinegar, 1 tablespoon oil and the sugar until they are well blended. Marinate the kidney strips in the sauce for 30 minutes.

Pour the stock into a pan. Add the beans, celery and butter. Stir-fry for 5 minutes over a moderate heat.

Heat the remaining oil in a frying pan (skillet) over a moderate heat. When the oil is hot, add the kidneys and marinade. Stir-fry for 1 minute. Push the kidney pieces to one side and pour the vegetables into the centre of the pan. When the contents come to the boil, stir-fry for a further 30 seconds. Transfer to a warmed serving dish. SERVES 4.

STIR-FRIED LAMBS' LIVER WITH LEEKS AND SPRING ONIONS (SCALLIONS)

METRIC/IMPERIAL	AMERICAN
450 g/1 lb lambs' liver, cut into thins strips	1 lb lambs' liver, cut into thin strips
2 tablespoons soy sauce*	2 tablespoons soy sauce*
1½ tablespoons hoisin sauce*	1½ tablespoons hoisin sauce*
1 teaspoon sugar	1 teaspoon sugar
1 teaspoon chilli sauce	1 teaspoon chili sauce
3 tablespoons vegetable oil	3 tablespoons vegetable oil
1 tablespoon cornflour	1 tablespoon cornstarch
2 tablespoons water	2 tablespoons water
2 tablespoons dry sherry	2 tablespoons dry sherry
2 medium leeks, cut into 2.5 cm/1 inch lengths	2 medium leeks, cut into 1 inch lengths
1 tablespoon lard	1 tablespoon shortening
3 spring onions, cut into 2.5 cm/1 inch lengths	3 scallions, cut into 1 inch lengths

Rub the liver with half the soy sauce, hoisin sauce, sugar, chilli sauce and 1 tablespoon of oil. Leave for 30 minutes. Blend together the cornflour (cornstarch), water and sherry until smooth.

Heat the remaining oil in a large frying pan (skillet) over a high heat. When the oil is hot, add the leeks and stir-fry for 1 minute. Push to one side of the pan.

Add the lard (shortening) and, when it has melted, add the liver, spring onions (scallions), the remaining marinade, and the remaining soy sauce, hoisin sauce, sugar and chilli sauce. Stir-fry for a further 1½ minutes. Stir the leeks into the liver and spring onion (scallion) mixture and cook for 1 minute. Add the cornflour (cornstarch) mixture and stir until the sauce thickens. Transfer to a warmed serving dish. SERVES 4.

Stir-Fried Lambs' Kidneys with Celery and French Beans

SIMMERED AND DEEP-FRIED LAMB

METRIC/IMPERIAL	AMERICAN
750 g–1 kg/1½–2 lb leg of lamb	1½–2 lb leg of lamb
vegetable oil for deep-frying	vegetable oil for deep-frying
½ medium cucumber, cut into matchstick strips	½ medium cucumber, cut into matchstick strips
3 slices root ginger, peeled and chopped	3 slices ginger root, peeled and chopped
4 spring onions, cut into 3.5 cm/1½ inch lengths	4 scallions, cut into 1½ inch lengths
Sauce:	Sauce:
1½ tablespoons soy sauce*	1½ tablespoons soy sauce*
1½ tablespoons soy paste*	1½ tablespoons soy paste*
1½ tablespoons hoisin sauce*	1½ tablespoons hoisin sauce*
1½ tablespoons plum sauce*	1½ tabelspoons plum sauce*
1½ tablespoons dry sherry	1½ tablespoons dry sherry
1½ teaspoons sugar	1½ teaspoons sugar

Combine all the sauce ingredients together until they are well blended.

Place the lamb in a flameproof casserole and cover with water. Bring to the boil, skimming any scum from the surface. Place the casserole in a preheated moderate oven, 180°C/350°F, Gas Mark 4, for 2½ hours, stirring a few times. Remove the lamb from the casserole and drain.

Heat the oil in a deep-fryer to 180°C/350°F. Gently lower the lamb into the pan and deep-fry for 8 to 9 minutes. Remove from the pan and drain on kitchen paper towels.

While still hot, cut the lamb into 1 cm/½ inch slices. Serve in toasted buns with cucumber strips, ginger and spring onions (scallions). Serve the sauce separately. SERVES 4.

STEWED LAMB WITH ORANGE

METRIC/IMPERIAL	AMERICAN
1 tablespoon soy sauce*	1 tablespoon soy sauce*
1 tablespoon dry sherry	1 tablespoon sherry
1 teaspoon ground ginger	1 teaspoon ground ginger
2 tablespoons finely grated orange rind	2 tablespoons finely grated orange rind
1 teaspoon salt	1 teaspoon salt
1 kg/2 lb lean meat, cut into 1 cm/½ inch cubes	2 lb boneless lamb for stew, cut into ½ inch cubes
1.2 litres/2 pints stock or water	5 cups stock or water
1 tablespoon cornflour	1 tablespoon cornstarch

Mix together the soy sauce, sherry, ginger, orange rind and salt. Add the lamb and mix well. Place the lamb mixture in a large pan with the stock or water. Bring to the boil, skim off the scum, cover and simmer for 2 hours.

Mix the cornflour (cornstarch) to a smooth paste with a little cold water and add to the pan. Return to the boil, stirring until slightly thickened. Serve hot. SERVES 6 to 8.

SHREDDED LAMB WITH ONIONS

METRIC/IMPERIAL	AMERICAN
1 garlic clove, crushed	1 garlic clove, crushed
1 tablespoon soy sauce*	1 tablespoon soy sauce*
1 tablespoon dry sherry	1 tablespoon dry sherry
150 ml/¼ pint chicken stock	⅔ cup chicken stock
1 tablespoon cornflour	1 tablespoon cornstarch
1 teaspoon salt	1 teaspoon salt
2 tablespoons peanut oil	2 tablespoons peanut oil
450 g/1 lb lean shoulder or leg of lamb, cut into thin strips	1 lb boneless lamb for stew, cut into thin strips
4 onions, sliced into rings	4 onions, sliced into rings

Stewed Lamb with Orange; Simmered and Deep-Fried Lamb; Woolly Lamb

Mix together the garlic, soy sauce, sherry, stock, cornflour (cornstarch) and salt until well blended.

Heat the oil in a wok or frying pan (skillet) and stir-fry the lamb until it changes colour. Stir the cornflour (cornstarch) mixture and add to the pan with the onions. Bring to the boil, stirring, cover and simmer for 2 or 3 minutes. Transfer to a warmed serving dish. SERVES 4.

WOOLLY LAMB

METRIC/IMPERIAL	AMERICAN
2 tablespoons peanut oil	2 tablespoons peanut oil
450 g/1 lb leg or shoulder of lamb, cut into thin slices	1 lb boneless lamb for stew, cut into thin slices
2 Chinese dried mushrooms, soaked in warm water for 30 minutes*	2 Chinese dried mushrooms, soaked in warm water for 30 minutes*
150 g/5 oz bamboo shoots, cut into thin strips*	$1\frac{1}{4}$ cup bamboo shoots, cut into thin strips*
1 carrot, cut into wedges	1 carrot, cut into wedges
1 onion, cut into wedges	1 onion, cut into wedges
$\frac{1}{2}$ teaspoon salt	$\frac{1}{2}$ teaspoon salt
300 ml/$\frac{1}{2}$ pint chicken stock	$1\frac{1}{4}$ cups chicken stock
1 tablespoon soy sauce*	1 tablespoon soy sauce*
$\frac{1}{2}$ teaspoon sugar	$\frac{1}{2}$ teaspoon sugar
2 tablespoons cornflour	2 tablespoons cornstarch
vegetable oil for deep-frying	vegetable oil for deep-frying
50 g/2 oz transparent noodles	$\frac{1}{2}$ cup cellophane noodles

Heat the peanut oil in a pan and fry the meat slices until they change colour. Drain the mushrooms, squeeze dry, discard the stems and slice. Pour off the excess oil from pan and add the vegetables, salt, stock, soy sauce, sugar and cornflour (cornstarch). Bring to the boil, cover and simmer, stirring constantly, for 5 minutes.

Heat the vegetable oil in a deep-fryer to 180°C/350°F. Loosen the noodles and deep-fry in the hot oil for 15 seconds or until they puff up. Drain well on kitchen paper towels. Serve the lamb mixture on a heated serving dish, topped with the noodles. SERVES 4.

Eggs

SCRAMBLED EGG AND MIXED VEGETABLES WITH SWEET AND SOUR SAUCE

METRIC/IMPERIAL	AMERICAN
2 tablespoons butter	2 tablespoons butter
$\frac{1}{4}$ chicken stock cube	1 chicken bouillon cube
4 tablespoons water	4 tablespoons water
1 medium cauliflower, divided into small florets	1 medium cauliflower, divided into small florets
2 celery sticks, cut into 1 cm/$\frac{1}{2}$ inch lengths	2 stalks celery, cut into $\frac{1}{2}$ inch lengths
2 tomatoes, cut into wedges	2 tomatoes, cut into wedges
1 red pepper, cored, seeded and diced	1 red pepper, cored, seeded and diced
100 g/4 oz bean sprouts*	2 cups bean sprouts*
1 tablespoon soy sauce*	1 tablespoon soy sauce*
3 tablespoons vegetable oil	3 tablespoons vegetable oil
4–5 eggs	4–5 eggs
1 teaspoon salt	1 teaspooon salt
freshly ground black pepper	freshly ground black pepper
450 g/1 lb hot cooked rice	6 cups hot cooked rice
Sauce:	Sauce:
1$\frac{1}{4}$ tablespoons sugar	1$\frac{1}{4}$ tablespoons sugar
2 tablespoons white wine vinegar	2 tablespoons white wine vinegar
1 tablespoon tomato purée	1 tablespoon tomato paste
1 tablespoon soy sauce*	1 tablespoon soy sauce*
3 tablespoons orange juice	3 tablespoons orange juice
1 tablespoon cornflour	1 tablespoon cornstarch,
4 tablespoons water	4 tablespoons water

Place the butter, crumbled stock (bouillon) cube and water into a saucepan. Heat gently until the butter has melted, then add the cauliflower, celery, tomatoes, pepper, bean sprouts and soy sauce. Stir-fry for 1 minute. Reduce the heat to fairly low, cover the pan and simmer for 3 to 4 minutes. Remove from the heat and keep hot.

Break the eggs into a bowl and sprinkle with salt and pepper. Heat the oil in a frying pan (skillet), then pour in the eggs, tilting the pan so that they spread out evenly. Cook without stirring for 1 minute. Remove from the heat and leave until the eggs are about to set. Gently stir a few times, being careful not to scramble. Remove from the heat and keep hot.

Mix together the sauce ingredients until they are well blended. Pour into a small saucepan and bring to the boil, stirring until the sauce thickens.

Arrange the cooked rice on a warmed serving dish. Place the eggs on top and surround with the vegetable mixture. Pour sauce over the top, and serve immediately. SERVES 4.

STIR-FRIED EGGS WITH SHREDDED HAM OR BACON

METRIC/IMPERIAL	AMERICAN
4–5 eggs	4–5 eggs
1 teaspoon salt	1 teaspoon salt
freshly ground black pepper	freshly ground black pepper
2 tablespoons vegetable oil	2 tablespoons vegetable oil
2 tablespoons butter	2 tablespoons butter
1–2 slices ham or 2–3 rashers bacon, cut into matchstick strips	1–2 slices ham or 2–3 slices bacon, cut into matchstick strips
3–4 spring onions, cut into thin rounds	3–4 scallions, cut into thin rounds
1 tablespoon dry sherry	1 tablespoon dry sherry

STEAMED BEAN CURD WITH EGG YOLKS

METRIC/IMPERIAL	AMERICAN
2–3 egg yolks or eggs	2–3 egg yolks or eggs
1½ teaspoons salt	1½ teaspoons salt
2 cakes bean curd, mashed*	2 cakes bean cured, mashed*
1 tablespoon cornflour	1 tablespoon cornstarch
½ chicken stock cube, dissolved in 150 ml/¼ pint hot stock	1 chicken bouillon cube, dissolved in ⅔ cup hot stock or broth
3 tablespoons vegetable oil	3 tablespoons vegetable oil
2 tablespoons lard or butter	2 tablespoons shortening or butter
2–3 tablespoons chopped ham	2–3 tablespoons chopped ham
3 tablespoons Chinese snow pickle* or gherkins	3 tablespoons Chinese snow pickle* or gherkins
3 tablespoons shelled peas	3 tablespoons shelled peas

Break the eggs or egg yolks into a bowl. Sprinkle with salt and add the bean curd. Beat until they are well blended. Add the cornflour (cornstarch) to the stock and blend well. Add to the egg and bean curd mixture and beat together until well blended.

Heat the oil and fat in a saucepan over a moderate heat then add the bean curd mixture. When the centre starts to bubble, pour into a heatproof bowl. Sprinkle evenly with the chopped ham, pickles and peas.

Place the bowl in a steamer and steam for 5 to 6 minutes. Remove from the heat and serve immediately. SERVES 4.

STEAMED EGGS WITH SPINACH

METRIC/IMPERIAL	AMERICAN
6 eggs, beaten	6 eggs, beaten
250 ml/8 fl oz hot water	1 cup hot water
1 teaspoon salt	1 teaspoon salt
2 teaspoons dry sherry	2 teaspoons pale dry sherry
50 g/2 oz spinach leaves	¾ cup spinach leaves
50 g/2 oz cooked ham, chopped	¼ cup chopped cooked ham
50 g/2 oz peeled prawns	1 large shrimp, peeled
To garnish:	For garnish:
1 tablespoon soy sauce*	1 tablespoon soy sauce*
1 teaspoon sesame seed oil*	1 teaspoon sesame seed oil*

Put the eggs in a heatproof bowl, add the water, salt and sherry and stir well.

Arrange the spinach, ham and prawns (shrimp) on top of the egg mixture, then lower the uncovered bowl into a large pan of boiling water.

Cover the pan, lower the heat so the water in the pan is just simmering and steam the eggs gently for 20 minutes. Sprinkle with the soy sauce and sesame oil. Serve hot. SERVES 4

Steamed Bean Curd with Egg Yolks; Scrambled Egg and Mixed Vegetables with Sweet and Sour Sauce; Stir-Fried Eggs with Shredded Ham or Bacon

Break the eggs into a bowl. Sprinkle with the salt and pepper and beat until they are well blended.

Heat the oil and fat in a frying pan (skillet) over a moderate heat then add the ham or bacon and half the spring onions (scallions). Stir and spread evenly over the pan. Pour the beaten eggs into the pan, tilting the pan so they spread out evenly. Cook without stirring for 1 minute.

Remove from the heat and leave until the eggs are just to set. Stir gently a few times. Return the pan to the heat. Sprinkle with the sherry and remaining spring onions (scallions). Cook until the mixture sizzles and serve immediately. SERVES 4.

VEGETABLE OMELETS WITH SWEET AND SOUR SAUCE

METRIC/IMPERIAL

4 Chinese dried mushrooms, soaked in warm water for 30 minutes*

3 celery sticks, sliced diagonally

4 eggs

1 tablespoon soy sauce*

salt

freshly ground black pepper

450 g/1 lb bean sprouts*

AMERICAN

4 Chinese dried mushrooms, soaked in warm water for 30 minutes*

3 stalks celery, sliced diagonally

4 eggs

1 tablespoon soy sauce*

salt

freshly ground black pepper

1 lb bean sprouts*

2 spring onions, cut into thin rounds

2 tablespoons vinegar

1 tablespoon sugar

1 tablespoon tomato purée

1 teaspoon cornflour

$\frac{1}{2}$ teaspoon finely chopped root ginger*

1 red pepper, cored, seeded and cut into wedges

2 pineapple rings, cut into wedges

2 tablespoons syrup from canned pineapple

2 tablespoons water

oil for frying

2 scallions, cut into thin rounds

2 tablespoons vinegar

1 tablespoon sugar

1 tablespoon tomato paste

1 teaspoon cornstarch

$\frac{1}{2}$ teaspoon finely chopped ginger root*

1 red pepper, cored, seeded and cut into wedges

2 pineapple rings, cut into wedges

2 tablespoons syrup from canned pineapple

2 tablespoons water

oil for frying

STEAMED EGGS WITH CRAB

METRIC/IMPERIAL	AMERICAN
6 eggs	6 eggs
450 ml/¾ pint chicken stock	2 cups chicken stock
1 teaspoon dry sherry	1 teaspoon dry sherry
1 tablespoon soy sauce*	1 tablespoon soy sauce*
½ tablespoon peanut oil	½ tablespoon peanut oil
100 g/4 oz chopped crab meat	½ cup chopped crab meat
salt	salt
freshly ground black pepper	freshly ground black pepper

Beat the eggs and stir in all the other ingredients. Pour into an oiled pudding basin (heatproof mixing bowl) and cover with greaseproof (waxed) paper and then a layer of foil. Tie down securely. Place in a steamer over gently simmering water for 30 to 40 minutes, or until set. (When cooked, the tip of a knife inserted into the eggs will come out clean.) Invert onto a hot serving dish and serve immediately. SERVES 4.

LIANG-FAR EGGS

METRIC/IMPERIAL	AMERICAN
2 Chinese dried mushrooms, soaked in warm water for 30 minutes*	2 Chinese dried mushrooms, soaked in warm water for 30 minutes*
2 teaspoons soy sauce*	2 teaspoons soy sauce*
1 tablespoon dry sherry	1 tablespoon dry sherry
½ teaspoon sugar	½ teaspoon sugar
150 ml/¼ pint chicken stock	⅔ cup chicken stock
1 tablespoon cornflour	1 tablespoon cornstarch
pinch of monosodium glutamate*	pinch of monosodium glutamate*
oil for frying	oil for frying
1 garlic clove, crushed	1 garlic clove, crushed
½ teaspoon salt	½ teaspoon salt
100 g/4 oz Chinese cabbage or spinach, finely shredded	1½ cups finely shredded bok choy or spinach
4 celery sticks, sliced diagonally	4 stalks celery, sliced diagonally
150 g/5 oz bamboo shoots, thinly sliced*	1¼ cups bamboo shoots, thinly sliced*
6 eggs	6 eggs
1 lettuce, for serving	1 head lettuce, for serving

Drain the mushrooms, squeeze dry and slice thinly, discarding the stems. Mix together the soy sauce, sherry, sugar, stock, cornflour (cornstarch) and monosodium glutmate until well blended.

Heat 1 tablespoon oil in a saucepan with the garlic and salt. Add the prepared vegetables and continue cooking, stirring, for 2 or 3 minutes. Stir the cornflour (cornstarch) mixture and add to the pan. Bring to the boil, stirring, and simmer for 2 to 3 minutes. Keep hot.

Heat about 5 cm/1 inch of oil in a small frying pan (skillet) and fry the eggs. Arrange the lettuce leaves on a serving dish. Arrange the eggs on top and pour the sauce over. SERVES 6.

Steamed Eggs with Crab

Drain the mushrooms, squeeze dry and slice thinly, discarding the stems. Cook the mushrooms and celery in boiling water for 3 minutes, then drain. Beat the eggs and add the soy sauce, salt, pepper and prepared vegetables.

In a small pan mix the vinegar, sugar, tomato purée (paste), cornflour (cornstarch) and ginger. Add the pepper and pineapple, pineapple syrup and water. Bring to the boil, stirring constantly, and simmer for 3 or 4 minutes.

Heat enough oil to cover the base of a small omelet pan (skillet). Add a generous tablespoon of the egg mixture and cook rapidly until lightly browned underneath. Place on a heated serving dish and keep hot. Continue to cook tablespoons of the egg mixture to make omelets. Serve with the sauce poured over. SERVES 4.

SCRAMBLED EGG AND BACON WITH QUICK-FRIED PEAS AND TOMATOES

METRIC/IMPERIAL	AMERICAN
4 eggs	4 eggs
1 teaspoon salt	1 teaspoon salt
freshly ground black pepper	freshly ground black pepper
4 tablespoons vegetable oil	4 tablespoons vegetable oil
1 medium onion, thinly sliced	1 medium onion, thinly sliced
3–4 rashers streaky bacon, cut into thin strips	3–4 slices bacon, cut into thin strips
1½ tablespoons butter	1½ tablespoons butter
225 g/8 oz shelled peas	1½ cups shelled peas
4–5 medium tomatoes, cut into quarters	4–5 medium tomatoes, cut into quarters
½ chicken stock cube	1 chicken bouillon cube
3 tablespoons boiling water	3 tablespoons boiling water
1½ tablespoons soy sauce*	1½ tablespoons soy sauce*
1½ teaspoons sugar	1½ teaspoons sugar
450 g/1 lb hot cooked rice	6 cups hot cooked rice

Break the eggs into a bowl and sprinkle with salt and pepper. Beat until they are well blended.

Heat the oil in a large frying pan (skillet) over a high heat. Add the onion and bacon and stir-fry for 1 minute. Pour on the beaten eggs, tilting the pan so they spread out evenly. Cook without stirring for 1 minute. Remove from the heat and leave until the eggs are just about to set, then stir gently a few times, being careful not to scramble them. Remove the egg mixture from the pan and keep hot.

Melt the butter in the pan and add the peas and tomatoes. Stir to blend. Sprinkle over the crumbled stock (bouillon) cube, water, soy sauce and sugar. Bring to the boil, then stir-fry for 30 seconds.

To serve, arrange the cooked rice on a warmed serving dish. Arrange the egg mixture on top and surround with the pea and tomato mixture. SERVES 4.

EGG-FLOWER MEAT

METRIC/IMPERIAL	AMERICAN
4 Chinese dried mushrooms, soaked in warm water for 30 minutes*	4 Chinese dried mushrooms, soaked in warm water for 30 minutes*
4 tablespoons lard	4 tablespoons shortening
2 spring onions, cut into 2.5 cm/1 inch lengths	2 scallions, cut into 1 inch lengths
100 g/4 oz lean pork, cut into thin strips	¼ lb lean pork, cut into thin strips
2 tablespoons soy sauce*	2 tablespoons soy sauce*
2 tablespoons stock	2 tablespoons stock
1 teaspoon sugar	1 teaspoon sugar
½ teaspoon salt	½ teaspoon salt
4 eggs	4 eggs
1 teaspoon sesame seed oil*	1 teaspoon sesame seed oil*
2 tablespoons medium or dry sherry	2 tablespoon cream or pale dry sherry

Drain the mushrooms, squeeze dry and slice thinly, discarding the stems.

Heat 2 tablespoons lard in a wok or frying pan (skillet) then add the spring onions (scallions), pork and mushrooms and stir-fry over a high heat for 1 minute. Add the soy sauce, stock, sugar and salt and stir-fry for another 1 minute. Remove the pan from the heat and keep warm.

Heat the remaining lard in another wok or frying pan (skillet) and add the eggs. Cook until nearly set, stir and turn and break up into small pieces.

Return the pan with the pork mixture to the heat and add the sesame seed oil. Stir-fry vigorously for 30 seconds then add the cooked eggs. Add the sherry and stir-fry gently for 30 seconds. Serve immediately. SERVES 4.

SWEET AND SOUR EGGS

METRIC/IMPERIAL	AMERICAN
150 ml/¼ pint chicken stock	⅔ cup chicken stock
1 garlic clove, crushed	1 garlic clove, crushed
1 tablespoon peanut oil	1 tablespoon peanut oil
2 tablespoons sugar	2 tablespoons sugar
2 tablespoons vinegar	2 tablespoons vinegar
1 teaspoon tomato purée	1 teaspoon tomato paste
½ teaspoon salt	½ teaspoon salt
1 tablespoon cornflour	1 tablespoon cornstarch
4 water chestnuts, thinly sliced*	4 water chestnuts, thinly sliced*
1 carrot, cut into wedges	1 carrot, cut into wedges
4 eggs	4 eggs
4 teaspoons water	4 teaspoons water
oil for frying	oil for frying

Mix together in a small saucepan the stock, garlic, peanut oil, sugar, vinegar, tomato purée (paste), salt and cornflour (cornstarch). Bring to the boil, stirring constantly, then add the vegetables and simmer for 4 to 5 minutes.

Beat each egg separately with 1 teaspoon of the water.

Heat a little oil in a small omelet pan (skillet) and make 4 omelets, one after the other. Fold the omelets and place on a warmed serving dish. Pour the sauce over and serve immediately. SERVES 4.

Egg-Flower Meat; Scrambled Egg and Bacon with Quick-Fried Peas and Tomatoes

Rice & Noodles

FRIED RICE WITH MIXED VEGETABLE SALAD

METRIC/IMPERIAL	AMERICAN
4 eggs	4 eggs
4 tablespoons vegetable oil	4 tablespoons vegetable oil
2 tablespoons butter	2 tablespoons butter
1 large onion, thinly sliced	1 large onion, thinly sliced
4 rashers streaky bacon, cut into matchstick strips	4 slices bacon, cut into matchstick strips
100 g/4 oz shelled peas	¾ cup shelled peas
450 g/1 lb hot cooked rice	6 cups hot cooked rice
1½ tablespoons soy sauce*	1½ tablespoons soy sauce*
Salad:	Salad:
2 slices root ginger, peeled and grated*	2 slices ginger root, peeled and grated*
1 garlic clove, crushed	1 garlic clove, crushed
2 spring onions, cut into thin rounds	2 scallions, cut into thin rounds
½ tablespoon soy sauce*	½ tablespoon soy sauce*
2 tablespoons wine vinegar	2 tablespoons wine vinegar
2 tablespoons stock	2 tablespoons stock
1½ teaspoons sugar	1½ teaspoons sugar
1 tablespoon sesame seed oil*	1 tablespoon sesame seed oil*
1 tablespoon olive oil	1 tablespoon olive oil
1 firm cos lettuce, shredded	1 firm romaine lettuce, shredded
100 g/4 oz bean sprouts*	2 cups bean sprouts*
2–3 tomatoes, cut into wedges	2–3 tomatoes, cut into wedges
2 celery sticks, cut into 2.5 cm/1 inch lengths	2 stalks celery, cut into 1 inch lengths
½ bunch watercress	½ bunch watercress

Break the eggs into a bowl and beat until well blended.

Heat the oil and butter in a large saucepan over a moderate heat. Add the onion and bacon and stir-fry for 1½ minutes. Pour the beaten eggs into one side of the pan and add the peas to the other. Cook without stirring for 1 minute. Remove from the heat and leave until the eggs are just about to set. Stir the eggs into the other ingredients in the pan. Return the pan to the heat. Stir in the cooked rice and sprinkle with the soy sauce. Keep hot.

Blend together the ginger, garlic, spring onions, soy sauce, wine vinegar, stock, sugar, sesame seed oil and olive oil to make a dressing. Place the lettuce, bean sprouts, tomatoes, celery and watercress in a bowl. Add the dressing and toss well.

To serve, arrange the fried rice on a warmed serving dish and spoon over the salad mixture. SERVES 4 to 6.

TEN-VARIETY CHOW MEIN

METRIC/IMPERIAL	AMERICAN
175 g/6 oz boned lean pork, shredded	¾ cup shredded pork loin
1 tablespoon soy sauce*	1 tablespoon soy sauce*
1 teaspoon sugar	1 teaspoon sugar
2 teaspoons cornflour	2 teaspoons cornstarch
350 g/12 oz egg noodles	¾ lb egg noodles
2 eggs	2 eggs
salt	salt
4 tablespoons vegetable oil	¼ cup vegetable oil
2 spring onions, cut into 2.5 cm/1 inch lengths	2 scallions, cut into 1 inch lengths
100 g/4 oz bamboo shoots, shredded*	1 cup shredded bamboo shoots*
100 g/4 oz fresh spinach leaves or other green vegetable, shredded	1½ cups shredded fresh spinach leaves or other green vegetable
100 g/4 oz peeled prawns	⅔ cup shelled shrimp
a little chicken stock or water (optional)	a little chicken stock or water (optional)

Ten-Variety Chow Mein

CHICKEN AND BACON CHOW MEIN WITH BEAN SPROUTS, MUSHROOMS AND SPRING ONIONS (SCALLIONS)

METRIC/IMPERIAL	AMERICAN
350 g/12 oz Chinese noodles or spaghetti	¾ lb Chinese noodles or spaghetti
6–8 medium Chinese dried mushrooms, soaked in warm water for 30 minutes*	6–8 medium Chinese dried mushrooms, soaked in warm water for 30 minutes*
3½ tablespoons vegetable oil	3½ tablespoons vegetable oil
3 rashers streak bacon, shredded	3 rashers bacon, shredded
1 medium onion, thinly sliced	1 medium onion, thinly sliced
2½ tablespoons soy sauce*	2½ tablespoons soy sauce*
½ chicken stock cube, dissolved	1 chicken bouillon cube, dissolved
4 tablespoons hot stock	4 tablespoons hot stock or broth
2½ tablespoons butter	2½ tablespoons butter
175 g/6 oz boned, shredded chicken breast	¾ cup boned, shredded chicken breast
6–8 button mushrooms, shredded	6–8 button mushrooms, shredded
100 g/4 oz bean sprouts*	2 cups bean sprouts*
3 spring onions, cut into 2.5 cm/1 inch lengths	3 scallions, cut into 1 inch lengths
1½ tablespoons dry sherry	1½ tablespoons dry sherry

Place the pork in a bowl with the soy sauce, sugar and cornflour (cornstarch). Mix well and leave to marinate for 20 minutes.

Cook the noodles in boiling water for 5 minutes, drain and rinse under cold running water, then drain again.

Beat the eggs with a little salt. Heat a little of the oil in a frying pan (skillet) over a low heat. Add the eggs and cook to make a thin omelet. Remove from the pan and cut into thin strips.

Heat a little more oil in the pan. Add the pork and stir-fry until it changes colour. Remove from the pan with a slotted spoon and drain.

Heat the remaining oil in the pan. Add the spring onions (scallions), bamboo shoots, spinach and a little salt. Stir then add the prawns (shrimp) and return the pork to the pan with the egg strips. Mix thoroughly, adding a little stock or water if necessary. Stir in the noodles and stir-fry until there is no liquid remaining in the pan. Transfer to a warmed serving dish and serve immediately. SERVES 4.

Cook the noodles in boiling, salted water for 7 to 8 minutes (spaghetti for 12 minutes) and drain. Rinse in cold water to keep separate. Drain the mushrooms, squeeze dry, discard the stems and slice.

Heat the oil in a large frying pan (skillet) over a moderate heat. Add the bacon, onion and dried mushrooms then stir-fry for 30 seconds. Cook for 1½ minutes and stir-fry again for 30 seconds.

Add the cooked noodles. Turn them thoroughly in the fat. Reduce the heat to low, sprinkle with 1¼ tablespoons soy sauce and 2 tablespoons stock. Stir and turn the noodles a few times, then cook for 2 minutes.

Meanwhile, heat the butter in a small frying pan (skillet) and add the chicken, fresh mushrooms, bean sprouts and spring onions (scallions). Stir-fry for 2 minutes. Sprinkle with the remaining soy sauce, stock and the sherry. Stir-fry for 30 seconds.

To serve, pour the noodles, dried mushrooms and bacon into a large, warmed serving bowl. Top with the chicken, mushrooms and spring onions (scallions). SERVES 4.

SHREDDED CHICKEN AND HAM SOUP NOODLES

METRIC/IMPERIAL	AMERICAN
350 g/12 oz Chinese noodles or spaghetti	¾ lb Chinese noodles or spaghetti
1 chicken stock cube	2 chicken bouillon cubes
900 ml/1½ pints clear stock	3¾ cups clear stock or broth
2 tablespoons vegetable oil	2 tablespoons vegetable oil
1 tablespoon butter	1 tablespoon butter
175–225 g/6–8 oz spinach, chopped	1½–2 cups chopped spinach
1 tablespoon soy sauce*	1 tablespoon soy sauce*
100 g/4 oz ham, shredded	½ cup shredded ham
100 g/4 oz roast chicken, shredded	½ cup shredded roast chicken

Cook the noodles in boiling salted water for 7 to 8 minutes (spaghetti for 12 minutes). Drain and rinse in cold water.

Add the crumbled stock cube (bouillon cubes) to the stock and bring to the boil. Add the noodles or spaghetti and simmer gently for 2 minutes.

Heat the oil and butter in a frying pan (skillet) over a high heat. Add the spinach, stir and turn for 1 minute. Sprinkle with the soy sauce and stir-fry for 1 minute.

Pour the noodles and soup into a large tureen and top with shredded ham, chicken and spinach. SERVES 4.

SZECHUAN NOODLES

METRIC/IMPERIAL	AMERICAN
100 g/4 oz peeled prawns, chopped	1 cup shelled, chopped shrimp
25 g/1 oz ham, shredded	¼ cup shredded ham
1 celery stick, chopped	1 stalk celery, chopped
50 g/2 oz minced cooked pork	¼ cup ground cooked pork
2 tablespoons peanut oil	2 tablespoons peanut oil
1 teaspoon finely chopped root ginger*	1 teaspoon finely chopped ginger root*
2 tablespoons brandy	2 tablespoons brandy
½ teaspoon chilli sauce	½ teaspoon chili sauce
1 tablespoon tomato sauce	1 tablespoon tomato sauce
1 tablespoon soy sauce*	1 tablespoon soy sauce*
1 tablespoon cornflour	1 tablespoon cornstarch
3 tablespoons chicken stock	3 tablespoons chicken stock
salt	salt
freshly ground black pepper	freshly ground black pepper
225 g/8 oz dried egg or home-made noodles (see page 74)	½ lb dried egg or home-made noodles (see page 74)

Mix together the prawns (shrimp), ham, celery and pork. Heat the oil in a frying pan (skillet) and add the pork mixture. Stir-fry for 3 to 4 minutes. Add the ginger, brandy, sauces, cornflour (cornstarch), stock, salt and pepper. Cook for 7 to 8 minutes, stirring constantly. Keep hot.

Cook the noodles in boiling salted water until tender. Drain and arrange on a warm serving dish. Pour the meat and vegetable mixture over. SERVES 4.

FRIED RICE WITH PORK AND SHRIMPS

METRIC/IMPERIAL	AMERICAN
2 tablespoons vegetable oil	2 tablespoons vegetable oil
2 spring onions, finely chopped	2 scallions, finely chopped
1 garlic clove, crushed	1 garlic clove, crushed
350 g/12 oz cooked rice	4 cups cooked rice
175 g/6 oz cooked pork, chopped	¾ cup chopped cooked pork
100 g/4 oz peeled shrimps	⅔ cup shelled shrimp
2 tablespoons soy sauce*	2 tablespoons soy sauce*
2 eggs	2 eggs
salt	salt
freshly ground black pepper	freshly ground black pepper

Heat the oil in a frying pan (skillet) and stir-fry the spring onions (scallions) and garlic in the hot oil for 2 minutes. Add the rice, mix well and heat through. Add the pork and shrimps with the soy sauce. Mix well together.

Beat the eggs and season with salt and pepper. Pour into the rice mixture in a thin stream, stirring all the time, until the eggs are cooked. Serve immediately. SERVES 4.

TEN-VARIETY FRIED RICE

Fried Rice with Pork and Shrimps; Szechuan Noodles;
Shredded Chicken and Ham Soup Noodles

METRIC/IMPERIAL

*3 Chinese dried mushrooms,
soaked in warm water for
30 minutes**

*225 /8 oz long-grain rice,
rinsed*

3 eggs

salt

3 tablespoon vegetable oil

*4–5 spring onions, finely
chopped*

100 g/4 oz peeled prawns

50 g/2 oz cooked ham, diced

*50 g/2 oz cooked chicken or
pork, diced*

*50 g/2 oz bamboo shoots,
diced**

25 g/1 oz shelled peas

*2 tablespoons soy sauce**

AMERICAN

*3 Chinese dried mushrooms,
soaked in warm water for
30 minutes**

1 cup long-grain rice, rinsed

3 eggs

salt

3 tablespoons vegetable oil

4–5 scallions, finely chopped

⅔ cup shelled shrimp

¼ cup diced cooked ham

*¼ cup diced cooked chicken or
pork*

*½ cup diced bamboo shoots**

¼ cup shelled peas

*2 tablespoons soy sauce**

Drain the mushrooms, squeeze dry, discard the stems and
dice the caps. Place the rice in a saucepan with enough cold
water to come 2.5 cm/1 inch above the surface of the rice.
Bring to the boil then stir once to prevent the rice sticking.
Cover with a tight-fitting lid, reduce the heat as low as
possible and cook for 15 to 20 minutes.

Beat the eggs with a little salt. Heat 1 tablespoon oil in a
frying pan (skillet) over a low heat. Add eggs and cook to
make an omelet. Remove from the pan and leave to cool.

Heat the remaining oil in the pan. Add the spring onions
(scallions), then stir in the prawns (shrimp), ham, chicken or
pork, mushrooms, bamboo shoots and peas. Add the soy
sauce and the cooked rice. Cook, stirring for 1 minute. Break
the omelet into pieces and fold into the rice mixture. Serve
immediately. SERVES 4.

NOODLE PASTE

METRIC/IMPERIAL	AMERICAN
225 g/8 oz plain flour	2 cups all-purpose flour
pinch of salt	pinch of salt
1 egg	1 egg

Sift the flour and salt into a mixing bowl. Make a well in the centre and add the egg. Using a round-bladed knife, mix the flour into the egg and add enough water to make a stiff dough. Knead with the hand very thoroughly. Roll out the dough as thinly as possible on a lightly floured board.
Hun t'un: cut into 7.5 cm/2 to 3 inch squares.
Dumplings: cut into 10 cm/4 inch diameter rounds.
Noodles: lightly flour the dough, roll up like a Swiss roll and slice into 1 mm to 3 mm/$\frac{1}{16}$ to $\frac{1}{8}$ inch slices. Unroll and hang over the back of a chair (on a clean tea towel) for about 20 minutes, to dry out.

Noodle Paste; Hun T'un with Spinach; Hun T'un with Chicken and Prawn Filling

HUN T'UN WITH SPINACH

METRIC/IMPERIAL	AMERICAN
450 g/1 lb belly of pork, minced	2 cups ground fresh pork sides
2 tablespoons soy sauce*	2 tablespoons soy sauce*
1 teaspoon brown sugar	1 teaspoon brown sugar
1 teaspoon salt	1 teaspoon salt
350 g/12 oz frozen leaf spinach, defrosted	$\frac{3}{4}$ lb frozen leaf spinach, defrosted
450 g/1 lb noodle paste (see previous recipe)	1 lb noodle paste (see previous recipe)
vegetable oil for deep-frying	vegetable oil for deep-frying

Mix the pork, soy sauce, sugar and salt together and leave for 10 minutes. Squeeze excess moisture from the spinach and add to the mixture. Mix well.

Cut out 5 cm/2 inch rounds from the noodle paste. Place a little of the meat mixture in the centre of each round, dampen the edges and press together to seal.

Heat the oil in a deep-fryer to 180°C/350°F. Drop in the hun t'un and fry until golden brown. Drain on kitchen paper towels and serve hot. SERVES 4 to 6.

WOR MEIN

METRIC/IMPERIAL	AMERICAN
225 g/8 oz dried egg or home-made noodles (see page 74)	½ lb dried egg or home-made noodles (see page 74)
2 Chinese dried mushrooms, soaked in warm water for 30 minutes*	2 Chinese dried mushrooms, soaked in warm water for 30 minutes*
2 tablespoons peanut oil	2 tablespoons peanut oil
175 g/6 oz lean pork, cut into thin strips	¾ cup lean pork strips
1 carrot, cut into wedges	1 carrot, cut into wedges
1 onion, cut into chunks	1 onion, cut into chunks
150 ml/¼ pint chicken stock	⅔ cup chicken stock
1 tablespoon cornflour	1 tablespoon cornstarch
1 tablespoon soy sauce*	1 tablespoon soy sauce*
salt	salt
6 hard-boiled eggs, quartered, to garnish	6 hard-cooked eggs, quartered, for garnish

Cook the noodles in salted boiling water for 15 to 20 minutes (home-made for 5 to 7 minutes) until soft. Drain and keep hot. Drain the mushrooms, squeeze dry and slice, discarding the stems.

Heat the oil in a saucepan. Add the pork and stir-fry until browned. Add the prepared vegetables, cover and cook gently for 10 minutes.

Mix together the stock, cornflour (cornstarch), soy sauce and salt. Add to the pan, bring to the boil, stirring and simmer for 1 to 2 minutes.

Arrange the noodles in 6 serving bowls. Put the pork mixture on top and serve garnished with quarters of hard-boiled egg. SERVES 6.

HUN T'UN WITH CHICKEN AND PRAWN FILLING

METRIC/IMPERIAL	AMERICAN
225 g/8 oz cooked chicken, minced	1 cup cooked ground chicken
225 g/8 oz peeled prawns, finely chopped	1 cup shelled chopped shrimp
2 spring onions, finely chopped	2 scallions, finely chopped
pinch of sugar	pinch of sugar
pinch of salt	pinch of salt
freshly ground black pepper	freshly ground black pepper
pinch of monosodium glutamate*	pinch of monosodium glutamate*
1 tablespoon soy sauce*	1 tablespoon soy sauce*
24 hun t'un squares, made from ½ recipe for noodle paste (see page 74)	24 hun t'un squares, made from ½ recipe for noodle paste (see page 74)
egg yolk	egg yolk
oil for deep-frying	oil for deep-frying
Pungent sauce:	Pungent sauce:
2 tablespoons sugar	2 tablespoons sugar
2 tablespoons vinegar	2 tablespoons vinegar
1 tablespoon soy sauce*	1 tablespoon soy sauce*
½ teaspoon finely chopped root ginger*	½ teaspoon finely chopped ginger root*
1 teaspoon tomato purée	1 teaspoon tomato paste
¼ teaspoon salt	¼ teaspoon salt
150 ml/¼ pint water	⅔ cup water
1 tablespoon cornflour	1 tablespoon cornstarch

Mix together the chicken, prawns (shrimp), spring onions (scallions), sugar, salt, pepper, monosodium glutamate and soy sauce.

Divide this filling mixture evenly between the paste squares. Spread the filling evenly over each square and roll it up like a Swiss roll, folding in the ends. Seal the edges with egg yolk.

Heat the oil in a deep-fryer to 180°C/350°F. Deep-fry the hun t'un until golden brown then drain on kitchen paper towels. Blend the sauce ingredients in a saucepan. Heat, stirring until the sauce comes to the boil, then simmer for 2 to 3 minutes. Serve the hun t'un hot with the pungent sauce. SERVES 6.

NOODLES IN SAUCE (BIRTHDAY LONG-LIFE NOODLES)

METRIC/IMPERIAL	AMERICAN
1-1.5 kg/2-3 lb knuckle of pork	2-3 lb ham hock
450 ml/¾ pint soy sauce*	2 cups soy sauce*
3 tablespoons dry sherry	3 tablespoons dry sherry
750 ml/1¼ pints clear stock	3 cups clear stock or broth
450 g/1 lb Chinese noodles	1 lb Chinese noodles
3-4 hard-boiled eggs	3-4 hard-cooked eggs

Put the knuckle (ham hock) into a flameproof casserole. Cover with water and bring to the boil. Cover and simmer gently for 40 minutes, skimming any scum from the surface. Add 3½ tablespoons soy sauce, and the sherry. Reduce the heat to very low and place an asbestos mat under the pan, or place the casserole in a preheated cool oven, 150°C/300°F, Gas Mark 2 for 1 hour. Add the stock and simmer gently for a further 1 hour.

Cook the noodles in boiling salted water for 7 to 8 minutes and drain. Remove the knuckle (ham hock) from the pan and scrape the meat from the bones. Add the noodles to the stock.

Shell the eggs and place in a pan with the remaining soy sauce. Simmer for 15 minutes, turning the eggs 5-6 times, until they are brown.

To serve, place the noodle mixture in a large serving bowl, and arrange the meat and eggs on top. SERVES 6 to 8.

CHOW MEIN WITH SEAFOOD

METRIC/IMPERIAL	AMERICAN
350 g/12 oz Chinese noodles or spaghetti	¾ lb Chinese noodles or spaghetti
3½ tablespoons vegetable oil	3½ tablespoons vegetable oil
1 medium onion, shredded	1 medium onion, shredded
2 rashers bacon, shredded	2 slices bacon, shredded
1 × 225 g/8 oz can clams or crab meat	1 × 8 oz can clams or crab meat
3 tablespoons soy sauce*	3 tablespoon soy sauce*
Garnish:	Garnish:
2½ tablespoons butter	2½ tablespoons butter
3 slices root ginger, peeled and shredded*	3 slices ginger root, peeled and shredded*
3 garlic cloves, crushed	3 garlic cloves, crushed
½ red pepper, cored, seeded and shredded	½ red pepper, cored, seeded and shredded
6 opened oysters	6 shucked oysters
225 g/8 oz peeled prawns or shelled mussels	½ lb shelled shrimp or mussels
3 spring onions, cut into 2.5 cm/1 inch lengths	3 scallions, cut into 1 inch lengths
salt	salt
freshly ground black pepper	freshly ground black pepper
1 teaspoon sugar	1 teaspoon sugar
2 tablespoons dry sherry	2 tablespoons dry sherry

Cook the noodles in boiling, salted water for 7 to 8 minutes (spaghetti for 12 minutes) then drain and rinse in cold water.

Heat the oil in a large frying pan (skillet) over a high heat. Add the onion and bacon and stir-fry for 1½ minutes. Add the clams or crab meat and 2 tablespoons of the soy sauce. Stir and turn in the fat for 1 minute. Pour in the noodles and spaghetti and sprinkle with the remaining soy sauce. Stir-fry for 1 minute. Reduce the heat to low and simmer gently for 3 to 4 minutes, until heated through.

Heat the butter in a small frying pan (skillet) over a high heat. When the butter has melted, add the ginger, garlic, pepper, oysters and prawns (shrimp). Stir-fry for 1 minute. Sprinkle with the spring onions (scallions), salt and pepper, sugar and sherry then stir-fry for 1 minute.

To serve, spoon the noodle mixture into a large serving bowl and pour over the seafood sauce as a garnish. SERVES 6 to 8.

CHOW MEIN WITH SHREDDED DUCK MEAT AND CELERY

METRIC/IMPERIAL	AMERICAN
225 g/8 oz Chinese noodles	½ lb Chinese noodles
3 tablespoon vegetable oil	3 tablespoons vegetable oil
3 celery sticks, shredded	3 stalks celery, shredded
1 teaspoon sugar	1 teaspoon sugar
1½ tablespoons soy sauce*	1½ tablespoons soy sauce*
100 g/4 oz roast duck meat, shredded	1 cup shredded roast duck meat
1 teaspoon chilli sauce	1 teaspoon chili sauce
2 tablespoons sherry	2 tablespoons sherry
1 tablespoon butter	1 tablespoon butter
4 tablespoons stock	4 tablespoons stock
1 slice root ginger, peeled and finely chopped*	1 slice ginger root, peeled and finely chopped*
1 tablespoon chopped parsley	1 tablespoon chopped parsley

Cook the noodles in boiling water for 6-7 minutes. Drain, then rinse under cold running water and reserve.

Heat 2 tablespoons oil in a wok or frying pan (skillet). Add the celery and stir-fry over a high heat for 1 minute. Add the sugar and soy sauce and stir-fry for 30 seconds. Add the duck meat, chilli sauce and 1 tablespoon of the sherry and stir-fry for 30 seconds. Remove the duck meat and celery from the pan with a slotted spoon and keep warm.

Add the remaining oil and the butter to the pan with the stock and ginger and melt the butter over a high heat. Add the noodles and stir-fry for 1 minute. Reduce the heat to low and stir-fry slowly for a further 2 minutes. Pour the noodle mixture into a hot serving dish.

Add the remaining sherry and the parsley to the pan over a high heat. Return the duck and celery to the pan and stir-fry for 30 seconds. Spoon over the noodles and serve. SERVES 4.

Chow Mein with Seafood

Vegetables

BEAN SPROUT SALAD

METRIC/IMPERIAL	AMERICAN
450 g/1 lb fresh bean sprouts	1 lb fresh bean sprouts
2 eggs	2 eggs
salt	salt
1 tablespoon vegetable oil	1 tablespoon vegetable oil
100 g/4 oz cooked ham, cut into thin strips	½ cup thinly sliced cooked ham
Sauce:	Sauce:
2 tablespoons soy sauce*	2 tablespoons soy sauce*
2 tablespoons vinegar	2 tablespoons vinegar
1 tablespoon sesame seed oil*	1 tablespoon sesame seed oil*
freshly ground black pepper	freshly ground black pepper
To garnish:	For garnish:
thinly pared strip of red pepper	thinly pared strip of red pepper
parsley sprig	parsley sprig

Cook the bean sprouts in boiling salted water for 3 minutes. Drain, rinse in cold water, then drain again and set aside.

Beat the eggs with a little salt. Heat the oil in a frying pan (skillet) over a low heat. Add the eggs and cook to make a thin omelet. Remove from the pan, leave to cool, then cut into thin strips.

Combine the sauce ingredients, then mix with the bean sprouts. Transfer to a serving dish, then arrange the ham and omelet strips on top. Garnish with the red pepper, coiled to resemble a flower head, with the parsley in the centre. Serve cold. SERVES 4.

KIDNEY FLOWER SALAD

METRIC/IMPERIAL	AMERICAN
350 g/12 oz pigs' kidneys, skinned and split in half lengthways	¾ lb pork kidney, skinned and split in half lengthwise
1 medium head celery, sliced diagonally	1 medium bunch celery, sliced diagonally
2 slices root ginger, peeled and finely shredded*	2 slices ginger root, peeled and finely shredded*
2 spring onions, finely chopped	2 scallions, finely chopped
Sauce:	Sauce:
2 tablespoons soy sauce*	2 tablespoons soy sauce*
1 tablespoon vinegar	1 tablespoon vinegar
1 tablespoon sesame seed oil*	1 tablespoon sesame seed oil*
1 teaspoon chilli sauce	1 teaspoon chili sauce
½ teaspoon sugar	½ teaspoon sugar
To garnish: (optional)	For garnish: (optional)
pineapple chunks	pineapple chunks
radish slices	radish slices
grapes	grapes

Kidney Flower Salad; Bean Sprout Salad

Score the surface of the kidneys in a criss-cross pattern, then cut them into pieces. Cook the kidneys in boiling water for 2 minutes. Drain, rinse in cold water, then drain again and transfer to a serving dish. Arrange the sliced celery around the kidneys.

Mix all the sauce ingredients together, then mix with half the ginger and the spring onions (scallions). Pour the sauce over the kidneys and leave to marinate for about 30 minutes before serving. Top with the remaining ginger. Garnish with the pineapple, raddish and grapes, if liked. Serve cold. SERVES 4.

CAULIFLOWER FU-YUNG

METRIC/IMPERIAL	AMERICAN
½ chicken stock cube, dissolved in 150 ml/¼ hot stock	1 chicken bouillon cube, dissolved in ⅔ cup hot broth
1 large cauliflower, divided into small florets	1 large cauliflower, divided into small florets
Fu-Yung:	Fu-Yung:
3 egg whites	3 egg whites
3–4 tablespoons minced chicken breast	3–4 tablespoons ground chicken breast
1 teaspoon salt	1 teaspoon salt
freshly ground black pepper	freshly ground black pepper
2 tablespoons milk	2 tablespoons milk
2 tablespoons cornflour	2 tablespoons cornstarch
2 tablespoons vegetable oil	2 tablespoons vegetable oil
2 tablespoons butter	2 tablespoons butter

Beat the egg whites, minced (ground) chicken, salt, pepper, milk and cornflour (cornstarch) together until the mixture is nearly stiff but not dry.

Heat the stock in a large saucepan over a moderate heat. Add the cauliflower and stir and turn for 3 to 4 minutes, until the liquid has almost evaporated.

Heat the oil and butter in a large frying pan (skillet) over a moderately low heat. When the butter has melted, add the beaten egg white mixture. Turn it in the fat for 1 minute. Pour in the cauliflower and increase the heat to high. Stir and turn the cauliflower in the egg white mixture for 1½ to 2 minutes, until well covered. Transfer to a hot serving dish.
SERVES 4.

HOT QUICK-FRIED SPINACH

METRIC/IMPERIAL	AMERICAN
3 tablespoons vegetable oil	3 tablespoons vegetable oil
2 tablespoons butter	2 tablespoons butter
1 teaspoon salt	1 teaspoon salt
3–4 garlic cloves, crushed	3–4 garlic cloves, crushed
450 g/1 lb spinach	1 lb spinach
1 tablespoon soy sauce*	1 tablespoon soy sauce*
1 teaspoon sugar	1 teaspoon sugar
1 tablespoon dry sherry	1 tablespoon dry sherry
1 tablespoon lard	1 tablespoon shortening

Heat the oil and butter in a large saucepan. When the butter has melted, add the salt and garlic. Stir and turn in the hot fat a few times. Pour in the spinach and increase the heat to high. Stir and turn in the fat quickly until every leaf is well coated. Sprinkle with the soy sauce, sugar and sherry. Stir-fry for 1 minute. Add the lard (shortening) to give the spinach a final floss and stir-fry in the melting fat a few times. Transfer to a hot serving dish. SERVES 4.

FRIED MUSHROOMS AND BAMBOO SHOOTS

METRIC/IMPERIAL	AMERICAN
12 Chinese dried mushrooms, soaked in warm water for 30 minutes*	12 Chinese dried mushrooms, soaked in warm water for 30 minutes*
2 tablespoons vegetable oil	2 tablespoons vegetable oil
225 g/8 oz bamboo shoots, sliced*	2 cups sliced bamboo shoots*
pinch of salt	pinch of salt
2 tablespoons medium or dry sherry	2 tablespoons cream or pale dry sherry
1 teaspoon soy sauce*	1 teaspoon soy sauce*
1 tablespoon cornflour	1 tablespoon cornstarch
100 g/4 oz minced ham	½ cup ground ham

Drain the mushrooms, reserving the liquid squeeze dry and slice, discarding the stems.

Heat the oil in a wok or frying pan (skillet) and stir-fry the mushrooms for 3 minutes. Remove from the pan. Add the bamboo shoots to the pan with the salt, sherry and soy sauce. Bring gently to the boil and simmer for 3 minutes.

Mix the cornflour (cornstarch) to a smooth paste with a little of the mushroom water, make up to 150 ml/¼ pint (⅔ cup) and add to the pan with the mushrooms. Cover and simmer for 10 minutes. Arrange on a large serving dish and sprinkle with the ham. SERVES 4.

HOT-TOSSED VEGETABLES

METRIC/IMPERIAL	AMERICAN
3½ tablespoons vegetable oil	3½ tablespoons vegetable oil
1 medium onion, thinly sliced	1 medium onion, thinly sliced
3 garlic cloves, crushed	3 garlic cloves, crushed
2 slices root ginger, peeled and shredded*	2 slices ginger root, peeled and shredded*
1½ teaspoons salt	1½ teaspoons salt
½ green pepper, cored, seeded and cut into matchstick strips	½ green pepper, cored, seeded and cut into matchstick strips
½ red pepper, cored, seeded and cut into matchstick strips	½ red pepper, cored, seeded and cut into matchstick strips
¼ medium cucumber, cut into matchstick strips	¼ medium cucumber, cut into matchstick strips
2 celery sticks, cut into 3.5 cm/1½ inch lengths	2 stalks celery, cut into 1½ inch lengths
2 spring onions, cut into 3.5 cm/1½ inch lengths	2 scallions, cut into 1½ inch lengths
3–4 lettuce leaves, chopped	3–4 lettuce leaves, chopped
225 g/8 oz bean sprouts*	4 cups bean sprouts*
1½ teaspoons sugar	1½ teaspoons sugar
2 tablespoons soy sauce*	2 tablespoons soy sauce*
¼ chicken stock cube, dissolved in 2 tablespoons hot stock	½ chicken bouillon cube dissolved in 2 tablespoons hot stock
1 tablespoon lemon juice	1 tablespoon lemon juice
1 tablespoon sesame seed oil*	1 tablespoon sesame seed oil*

Heat the oil in a large wok or frying pan (skillet) over a moderate heat. Add the onion, garlic, ginger and salt and stir-fry for 30 seconds.

Add all the other vegetables. Increase the heat to high, stir and turn the vegetables until they are well coated. Sprinkle with the sugar, soy sauce and chicken stock. Stir-fry for 1½ minutes. Sprinkle with the lemon juice and sesame seed oil and stir once more. Serve hot. SERVES 4.

QUICK-BRAISED CABBAGE

METRIC/IMPERIAL	AMERICAN
700 g/1½ lb small green cabbage	6 cups cabbage
3 cloves garlic, crushed	3 cloves garlic, crushed
3½ tablespoons vegetable oil	3½ tablespoons vegetable oil
2 teaspoons salt	2 tablespoons salt
½ chicken stock cube dissolved in 4 tablespoons hot stock	½ chicken bouillon cube dissolved in 4 tablespoons hot stock
1 tablespoon lard	1 tablespoon shortening

Discard any coarse or discoloured outer leaves from the cabbage. Cut the heart into quarters or sixes. Clean thoroughly and pat dry.

Heat the oil in a saucepan over moderate heat. When the oil is hot, add the greens. Stir-fry for 1½ minutes until every leaf is well coated. Sprinkle with the salt, garlic and stock. Stir and turn a few times. Cook for 3–4 minutes. Add the lard (shortening) and stir and turn a few more times. Turn into a warmed serving dish and serve immediately. SERVES 4 to 6.

Hot-Tossed Vegetables

QUICK-FRIED GREEN BEANS
IN ONION AND GARLIC
SAUCE

METRIC/IMPERIAL	AMERICAN
½ chicken stock cube	1 chicken bouillon cube
150 ml/¼ pint hot stock	⅔ cup hot stock
450 g/1 lb French beans, topped and tailed	1 lb green beans, topped and tailed
3 tablespoons vegetable oil	3 tablespoons vegetable oil
1½ tablespoons butter	1½ tablespoons butter
4–6 garlic cloves, crushed	4–6 garlic cloves, crushed
1 teaspoon salt	1 teaspoon salt
2 spring onions, cut into thin rounds	2 scallions, cut into thin rounds
1 tablespoon soy sauce*	1 tablespoon soy sauce*
1 teaspoon sugar	1 teaspoon sugar
1 tablespoon dry sherry	1 tablespoon dry sherry

Dissolve the stock (bouillon) cube in the stock in a large saucepan. Add the beans and simmer until most of the liquid has evaporated, turning them constantly.

Heat the oil and butter in a large wok or frying pan (skillet) over a moderate heat. Add the garlic, salt and spring onions (scallions), and stir-fry for 30 seconds. Add the beans, stir and turn them in the fat until they are well coated. Sprinkle with soy sauce, sugar and sherry, then stir-fry for 1 minute. Transfer to a hot serving dish. SERVES 4.

RED-COOKED CABBAGE

METRIC/IMPERIAL	AMERICAN
½ chicken stock cube	1 chicken bouillon cube
5–6 tablespoons hot water	5–6 tablespoons hot water
2 tablespoons soy sauce*	2 tablespoons soy sauce*
1½ teaspoons sugar	1½ teaspoons sugar
freshly ground black pepper	freshly ground black pepper
2½ tablespoons vegetable oil	2½ tablespoons vegetable oil
1½ tablespoons lard or butter	1½ tablespoons shortening or butter
1 medium cabbage, cut into 2.5 cm/1 inch slices	1 medium cabbage, cut into 1 inch slices

Dissolve the stock (bouillon) cube in the water and mix with the soy sauce, sugar and pepper until well blended.

Heat the oil and fat in a saucepan over a moderate heat. When the fat has melted, add the cabbage and stir and turn in the hot fat until well coated. Sprinkle the soy sauce mixture evenly over the cabbage and stir several times. Reduce the heat to very low, cover and simmer for 18 to 20 minutes, stirring every 4 or 5 minutes. Transfer to a hot serving dish. SERVES 4.

QUICK-FRIED HOT-BRAISED BROCCOLI WITH CRAB MEAT

METRIC/IMPERIAL	AMERICAN
4½ tablespoons vegetable oil	4½ tablespoons vegetable oil
1 onion, finely chopped	1 onion, finely chopped
450 g/1 lb broccoli, divided into small florets	1 lb broccoli, divided into small florets
1 teaspoon salt	1 teaspoon salt
freshly ground black pepper	freshly ground black pepper
4 tablespoons stock	¼ cup stock
1 teaspoon chilli sauce	1 teaspoon chili sauce
2 tablespoons sherry	2 tablespoons sherry
4–5 tablespoons crab meat	4–5 tablespoons crab meat
½ tablespoon finely chopped spring onion	½ tablespoon finely chopped scallion
1 garlic clove, crushed	1 garlic clove, crushed

Heat 3 tablespoons oil in a saucepan, add the onion and stir-fry over a high heat for a few seconds. Add the broccoli, salt and pepper and stir-fry for 2 minutes. Add the stock, chilli sauce and sherry. Turn the vegetables once in the sauce and then cover the pan. Cook over a low heat for 3½ minutes.

Heat the remaining oil in a wok or frying pan (skillet), add the crab meat, spring onion (scallion) and garlic. Stir-fry for 1 minute over a high heat.

To serve, pour the broccoli and sauce into deep-sided serving dish and top with the crab meat. SERVES 4.

Quick-Fried Green Beans in Onion and Garlic Sauce; Quick-Fried Hot-Braised Broccoli with Crab Meat

VEGETABLES WITH SWEET AND SOUR SAUCE

METRIC/IMPERIAL	AMERICAN
1 small red pepper, cored, seeded and cut into wedges	1 small red pepper, cored, seeded and cut into wedges
1 small green pepper, cored, seeded and cut into wedges	1 small green pepper, cored, seeded and cut into wedges
1 onion, cut into wedges	1 onion, cut into wedges
1 carrot, cut into wedges	1 carrot, cut into wedges
2 celery sticks, sliced diagonally	2 stalks celery, sliced diagonally
1 tablespoon cornflour	1 tablespoon cornstarch
1 tablespoon soy sauce*	1 tablespoon soy sauce*
4 tablespoons brown sugar	¼ cup firmly packed brown sugar
50 ml/¼ pint chicken stock	⅔ cup chicken stock
4 tablespoons vinegar	¼ cup vinegar
salt	salt

Drop the vegetables into boiling water and simmer for 5 minutes. Mix the cornflour (cornstarch) with the soy sauce until well blended.

Place the sugar, stock and vinegar in a saucepan, bring to the boil, then add the cornflour (cornstarch) mixture. Simmer, stirring, for 2 to 3 minutes until thickened. Add the vegetables and salt to taste and reheat. Transfer to a hot serving dish. SERVES 4.

CAULIFLOWER, WATER CHESTNUTS AND MUSHROOMS

METRIC/IMPERIAL	AMERICAN
1 small cauliflower, divided into florets	1 small cauliflower, divided into florets
6 Chinese dried mushrooms, soaked in warm water for 30 minutes*	6 Chinese dried mushrooms, soaked in warm water for 30 minutes*
2 tablespoons vegetable oil	2 tablespoons vegetable oil
8 water chestnuts, cut into large pieces*	8 water chestnuts, cut into large pieces*
2 tablespoons cornflour	2 tablespoons cornstarch
2 tablespoons soy sauce*	2 tablespoons soy sauce*
2 tablespoons medium or dry sherry	2 tablespoons cream or pale dry sherry
2 tablespoons stock	2 tablespoons stock

Cover the cauliflower with boiling water and leave for 5 minutes, then drain. Drain the mushrooms, reserving the liquid, squeeze dry and slice thinly, discarding the stems.

Heat the oil in a wok or frying pan (skillet). Stir-fry the mushrooms for 2 to 3 minutes over a high heat. Add the chestnuts and cauliflower, mix well and cook for 2 minutes.

Mix the cornflour (cornstarch) to a smooth paste with the remaining ingredients and add the mushroom liquid. Add to the pan and bring to the boil, stirring, until the mixture is thickened. Cook for 2 to 3 minutes and serve in a warmed serving dish. SERVES 4.

CHINESE PICKLED CUCUMBER

METRIC/IMPERIAL	AMERICAN
2 tablespoons vinegar	2 tablespoons vinegar
1 tablespoon brown sugar	1 tablespoon brown sugar
1 teaspoon ground ginger	1 teaspoon ground ginger
1 cucumber, peeled and thinly sliced	1 cucumber, peeled and thinly sliced
1 teaspoon sesame seed oil (optional)*	1 teaspoon sesame seed oil (optional)*

Place the vinegar, sugar and ginger in a small pan and bring to the boil. Pour over the cucumber in a bowl and leave until cold. Stir in sesame seed oil, if using, just before serving. SERVES 4.

SWEET AND SOUR CABBAGE

METRIC/IMPERIAL	AMERICAN
3 tablespoons vegetable oil	3 tablespoons vegetable oil
1 tablespoon butter	1 tablespoon butter
1 Chinese or Savoy cabbage, shredded	1 bok choy or Savoy cabbage, shredded
1 teaspoon salt	1 teaspoon salt
Sauce:	Sauce:
1½ tablespoons cornflour	1½ tablespoons cornstarch
5 tablespoons water	5 tablespoons water
1½ tablespoons soy sauce*	1½ tablespoons soy sauce*
2½ tablespoons sugar	2½ tablespoons sugar
3½ tablespoons vinegar	3½ tablespoons vinegar
3½ tablespoons orange juice	3½ tablespoons orange juice
2½ tablespoons tomato purée	2½ tablespoons tomato paste
1½ tablespoons medium or dry sherry	1½ tablespoons cream or pale dry sherry

Heat the oil and butter in a large saucepan over a high heat. Add the cabbage and sprinkle with salt. Stir-fry for 2 minutes. Reduce the heat to low and simmer gently for 5 to 6 minutes.

Mix the sauce ingredients together until well blended. Place the mixture in a small saucepan and simmer for 4 to 5 minutes, stirring constantly, until the liquid thickens and becomes translucent. Spoon the cabbage into a deep serving dish and pour the sauce over. SERVES 4 to 6.

Chinese Pickled Cucumber; Cauliflower, Water Chestnuts and Mushrooms

BEAN CURD WITH OYSTER SAUCE

METRIC/IMPERIAL	AMERICAN
2 tablespoons vegetable oil	2 tablespoons vegetable oil
100 g/4 oz mushrooms, sliced	1 cup sliced mushrooms
450 g/1 lb bean curd, broken inmall pieces*	1 lb bean curd, broken into small pieces*
3 tablespoons oyster sauce*	3 tablespoons oyster sauce*
pinch of freshly ground black pepper	pinch of freshly ground black pepper

Heat the oil in a wok or frying pan (skillet) and stir-fry the mushrooms over a high heat for 2 minutes. Remove them from the pan. Add the bean curd and cook gently for 2 to 3 minutes until browned on the outside. Add the oyster sauce and pepper, mix well and leave for 2 minutes. Add the mushrooms, mix well and gently heat through. Transfer to a warmed serving dish. SERVES 4.

COLD CUCUMBER

METRIC/IMPERIAL	AMERICAN
1 cucumber	1 cucumber
$\frac{1}{2}$ teaspoon salt	$\frac{1}{2}$ teaspoon salt
1 tablespoon soy sauce*	1 tablespoon soy sauce*
1 tablespoon wine vinegar	1 tablespoon wine vinegar
1 tablespoon caster sugar	1 tablespoon powdered sugar
2 teaspoons sesame oil*	2 teaspoons sesame oil*

Peel the cucumber carefully and cut into small dice. Sprinkle with the salt, soy sauce, wine vinegar, sugar and sesame oil. Leave to stand for 5 minutes, or until sugar has completely dissolved, before serving.

Braised Cabbage with Mushrooms; Bean Curd with Oyster Sauce; Cold Cucumber

BRAISED CABBAGE WITH MUSHROOMS

METRIC/IMPERIAL	AMERICAN
2 tablespoons peanut oil	2 tablespoons peanut oil
450 g/1 lb white or Chinese cabbage, roughly chopped	1 lb white cabbage or bok choy, roughly chopped
1 green pepper, cored, seeded and cut into strips	1 green pepper, cored, seeded and cut into strips
1 tablespoon soy sauce*	1 tablespoon soy sauce*
1 teaspoon sugar	1 teaspoon sugar
pinch of monosodium glutamate*	pinch of monosodium glutamate*
100 g/4 oz button mushrooms	1 cup button mushrooms
salt	salt
freshly ground black pepper	freshly ground black pepper
4 tablespoons water	¼ cup water

Heat the oil in a saucepan, add the cabbage and stir-fry for 2 to 3 minutes. Add the green pepper to the pan with the soy sauce, sugar, monosodium glutamate and mushrooms. Add salt and pepper to taste and the water. Cover the pan and cook for 5 to 7 minutes, shaking the pan occasionally. Transfer to a warmed serving dish. SERVES 4.

Desserts

STEAMED DUMPLINGS WITH SWEET FILLING

METRIC/IMPERIAL	AMERICAN
Pastry:	Pastry:
1½ tablespoons dried yeast	1½ tablespoons active dry yeast
2½ teaspoons sugar	2½ teaspoons sugar
3 tablespoons lukewarm water	3 tablespoons lukewarm water
450 g/1 lb plain flour	4 cups all-purpose flour
300 ml/½ pint lukewarm milk	1¼ cups lukewarm milk
Filling:	Filling:
1 × 225 g/8 oz can sweetened chestnut purée or yellow bean sauce*	1 × 8 oz can chestnut purée or yellow bean sauce*

Dissolve the yeast and sugar in the water. Sift the flour into a large bowl, then gradually stir in the yeast mixture and the milk. Mix to a firm dough. Turn the dough onto a lightly floured surface and knead well for at least 5 minutes. Transfer to a bowl, cover with a damp cloth and leave in a warm place for 1½ to 2 hours or until the dough has doubled in size.

Knead the dough on a lighly floured surface for about 5 minutes, then roll into a long sausage shape 5 cm/2 inches in diameter. Slice with a sharp knife into 2.5 cm/1 inch rounds. Flatten each round with the palm of the hand, then roll out to circles 10 cm/4 inches diameter.

Place 1 teaspoon chestnut purée or bean sauce in the centre of each round, then gather up the dough around the filling to meet at the top. Twist the top to enclose the filling tightly. Leave to rest for at least 20 minutes.

Place the dumplings on a damp cloth in the bottom of a steamer, leaving a 2.5 cm/1 inch space between each one. Steam for 15 to 20 minutes. Serve hot. MAKES ABOUT 24.

Sweet Bean Paste Pancakes; Plum Blossom and Snow Competing for Spring

PLUM BLOSSOM AND SNOW COMPETING FOR SPRING

METRIC/IMPERIAL	AMERICAN
2 dessert apples, peeled, cored and thinly sliced	2 dessert apples, peeled, cored and thinly sliced
2 bananas, peeled and thinly sliced	2 bananas, peeled and thinly sliced
juice of ½ lemon	juice of ½ lemon
2 eggs, separated	2 eggs, separated
100 g/4 oz sugar	½ cup sugar
3 tablespoons milk	3 tablespoons milk
3 tablespoons water	3 tablespoons water
3 tablespoons cornflour	3 tablespoons cornstarch

Arrange the apple and banana slices in alternate layers on an ovenproof dish, sprinkling each layer with lemon juice.

Place the egg yolks in a pan with the sugar, milk, water and cornflour (cornstarch). Blend until smooth then heat very gently, stirring, until the sauce thickens. Pour over the fruit.

Beat the egg whites until stiff, then spoon over the fruit. Bake in a preheated hot oven, 220°C/425°F, Gas Mark 7 for 5 minutes, until the top is crisp and golden. Serve hot or cold. SERVES 4.

SWEET BEAN PASTE PANCAKES (CRÊPES)

METRIC/IMPERIAL	AMERICAN
100 g/4 oz plain flour	1 cup all-purpose flour
1 egg, beaten	1 egg, beaten
150 ml/¼ pint water	⅔ cup water
6–8 tablespoons sweet red bean paste*, or finely chopped dates	6–8 tablespoons sweet red bean paste*, or finely chopped dates
vegetable oil for deep-frying	vegetable oil for deep-frying

Sift the flour into a large bowl, make a well in the centre and add the egg. Add the water gradually, beating constantly to make a smooth batter.

Lightly oil a 18 cm/7 inch frying pan (skillet) and place over a moderate heat. When the pan is very hot, pour in just enough batter to cover the bottom thinly, tilting the pan to spread it evenly. Cook for 30 seconds or until the underside is just firm, then carefully remove from the pan. Repeat with the remaining batter to make 6 to 8 pancakes (crêpes).

Divide the sweet red bean paste or dates equally between the pancakes (crêpes), placing the filling in the centre of the uncooked side of each one. Fold the bottom edge over the filling, then fold the sides towards the centre, to form an envelope. Brush the edge of the top flap with a little water, fold down and press the edges together firmly to seal.

Heat the oil in a deep-fryer to 180°C/350°F and deep-fry the pancakes (crêpes) for 1 minute or until crisp and golden. Remove and drain on kitchen paper towels. Cut each pancake (crêpe) into 6 or 8 slices and serve hot. SERVES 6.

ALMOND JELLY WITH CHOW CHOW

METRIC/IMPERIAL	AMERICAN
4 tablespoons gelatine	4 tablespoons unflavored gelatin
450 ml/¾ pint water	2 cups water
450 ml/¾ pint milk	2 cups milk
3½ tablespoons sugar	3½ tablespoons sugar
1 teaspoon almond essence	1 teaspoon almond extract
1 large or 2 small cans chow chow*	1 large or 2 small cans chow chow*

Soften the gelatine in 120 ml/4 fl oz (½ cup) water in a heatproof bowl placed over a saucepan of hot water. Stir until dissolved.

Heat the remaining water with the milk, sugar and almond essence (extract), stirring until dissolved. Stir in the gelatine and mix well.

Pour the mixture into a lightly oiled rectangular pan and leave until cooled and set.

To serve, cut the almond jelly into triangular or rectangular bite-size pieces. Arrange in a large bowl and pour the chow chow into the centre. Chill before serving. SERVES 4 to 6.

CARAMEL APPLES

METRIC/IMPERIAL	AMERICAN
6 medium apples, peeled, cored and quartered	6 medium apples, peeled, cored and quartered
6 tablespoons plain flour	6 tablespoons all-purpose flour
1 tablespoon cornflour	1 tablespoon cornstarch
2 egg whites	2 egg whites
vegetable oil for deep-frying	vegetable oil for deep-frying
100 g/4 oz sugar	½ cup sugar
2 tablespoons water	2 tablespoons water
1 tablespoon sesame seeds	1 tablespoon sesame seeds
1 tablespoon vegetable oil	1 tablespoon vegetable oil

Dust the apples lightly with a little of the flour. Sift the remaining flour and cornflour (cornstarch) into a bowl add the egg whites and mix to a paste.

Heat the oil in a deep-fryer to 180°C/350°F. Dip the apple quarters, one at a time, in the batter then carefully drop them into the oil. Fry until golden brown. Remove and drain on kitchen paper towels.

Place the sugar in a small saucepan with the water. Heat, stirring, until the sugar has caramelized and is a light golden brown. Stir in the apple quarters and sesame seeds. Serve in individual, lightly oiled dishes. SERVES 4.

Eight Precious Rice Pudding; Almond Biscuits; Almond Jelly with Chow Chow

ALMOND BISCUITS

METRIC/IMPERIAL	AMERICAN
350 g/12 oz plain flour	3 cups all-purpose flour
2 teaspoons baking powder	2 teaspoons baking powder
salt	salt
100 g/4 oz margarine or butter	½ cup margarine or butter
225 g/8 oz granulated sugar	1 cup firmly packed sugar
1 egg	1 egg
1 teaspoon almond essence	1 teaspoon almond extract
blanched almonds for decoration	blanched almonds for decoration
beaten egg, to glaze	beaten egg, for glazing

Sift the flour, baking powder and salt into a bowl. Cream the margarine or butter and sugar together until light and fluffy. Beat in the egg and almond essence (extract). Stir in the flour to make a stiff dough.

Form the mixture into balls about 2.5 to 3.5 cm/1 to 1½ inches in diameter and place on a greased baking sheet. Place half an almond (split lengthways) on each ball and press to flatten slightly. Brush with beaten egg.

Bake in a preheated moderate oven, 180°C/350°F, Gas Mark 4 for 20 minutes, or until golden. Cool on a wire rack. MAKES ABOUT 45.

EIGHT PRECIOUS RICE
PUDDING

METRIC/IMPERIAL	AMERICAN
750 g/1½ lb glutinous rice*	4 cups glutinous rice*
4–5 tablespoons lard	4–5 tablespoons shortening
150 g/5 oz crystallized fruits (dried lychees, dates, raisins, preserved ginger, prunes, cherries and mixed fruit)	1 cup candied fruit (dried lychees, dates, raisins, preserved ginger, prunes, cherries and mixed fruit)
4–5 tablespoons chopped nuts (almonds, chestnuts, walnuts etc)	4–5 tablespoons chopped nuts (almonds, chestnuts, walnuts etc)
5 tablespoons sugar	5 tablespoons sugar
7–8 tablespoons sweetened bean curd cheese*	7–8 tablespoons sweetened bean curd cheese*

Place the rice in a saucepan, cover with water and bring to the boil. Reduce the heat, cover tightly and cook for 10 to 15 minutes, or until all the water is absorbed. Remove from the heat and set aside.

Generously grease a heatproof bowl with ⅔ of the lard (shortening). Stick the crystallized (candied) fruit and nuts into the lard, pushing them against the sides and over the bottom of the bowl. Add the sugar and remaining lard to the rice and mix well. Spoon half the rice into the bowl, levelling off the top.

Spoon the bean curd cheese on top of the rice, then cover with the remaining rice, leaving a 1 cm/½ inch space at the top. Seal the top of the basin with foil or greaseproof (waxed) paper tied securely with string. Steam for 1½ hours.

To serve, remove the foil or paper and invert the pudding onto a warmed serving dish. SERVES 4 to 6.

ALMOND LAKE WITH MANDARIN ORANGES

METRIC/IMPERIAL	AMERICAN
600 ml/1 pint milk	2½ cups milk
100 g/4 oz granulated sugar	½ cup sugar
1 teaspoon almond essence	1 teaspoon almond extract
rice	⅓ cup ground rice
1 × 300 g/11 oz can mandarin oranges, drained	1 × 11 oz can mandarin oranges
25 g/1 oz flaked toasted almonds	¼ cup flaked toasted almonds

Put the milk, sugar, essence (extract) and rice in a saucepan. Bring to the boil, stirring constantly, and simmer for 5 minutes. Pour into a dish, cover and cool.

Spoon the rice into individual dishes. Place the mandarin oranges on the rice and sprinkle with the almonds before serving. SERVES 4.

JUJUBE CAKES

METRIC/IMPERIAL	AMERICAN
225 g/8 oz jujubes* or dates	½ lb jujubes* or dates
225 g/8 oz glutinous rice flour*	2 cups glutinous rice flour*

Put the jujubes in a pan, cover with cold water and bring to the boil. Simmer for 1 hour or until soft. Drain, then remove the skins and stones (pits). If using dates, remove the stones (pits) and heat slightly to soften the fruit.

Beat the fruit to form a paste. Add the rice flour and knead to make a soft dough. Roll out to 5 mm/¼ inch thick and cut out small shapes, using fancy cutters. Steam the cakes over a pan of boiling water for 5 minutes. MAKES ABOUT 24.

GINGERED FRUIT

METRIC/IMPERIAL	AMERICAN
1 × 425 g/15 oz can pineapple pieces, drained	1 × 15 oz can pineapple pieces, drained
1 × 300 g/11 oz can lychees, drained	1 × 11 oz can lychees, drained
1 tablespoon chopped glacé cherries	1 tablespoon chopped glacé cherries
2 tablespoons chopped crystallized ginger	2 tablespoons chopped candied ginger
25 g/1 oz flaked toasted almonds	¼ cup flaked toasted almonds

Mix together the pineapple, lychees, cherries and ginger in a mixing bowl. Chill well. Sprinkle the almonds over the top and serve immediately in small bowls. SERVES 6.

MOW FLOWER TWISTS

METRIC/IMPERIAL	AMERICAN
225 g/8 oz plain flour	2 cups all-purpose flour
100 g/4 oz butter	½ cup butter
100 g/4 oz granulated sugar	½ cup sugar
25 g/1 oz ground almonds	¼ cup ground almonds
1 egg	1 egg
½ teaspoon almond essence	½ teaspoon almond extract
vegetable oil for deep-frying	vegetable oil for deep-frying
icing sugar	confectioners' sugar

Sift the flour into a bowl and rub the butter with the fingertips until the mixture resembles breadcrumbs. Stir in the sugar and ground almonds. Add the egg and almond essence (extract) and knead well to make a pliable dough, adding a little water is necessary.

Roll the dough into a sausage shape 2.5 cm/1 inch in diameter and cut into 2.5 cm/1 inch lengths. Roll each piece into a ribbon about 23 to 25 cm/9 to 10 inches long, fold in half and twist twice. Take the ends of the ribbon back to the fold and push through the loop.

Heat the oil in a deep-fryer to 180°C/350°F. Deep-fry the twists until golden. Drain on kitchen paper towels and sprinkle with icing (confectioner) sugar. Serve cold. MAKES ABOUT 20.

STEAMED HONEYED PEARS

METRIC/IMPERIAL	AMERICAN
4 medium pears, peeled but with stems intact	4 medium pears, peeled but with stems intact
4 tablespoons sugar	4 tablespoons sugar
4 tablespoons clear honey	4 tablespoons clear honey
2 tablespoons sweet liqueur (Chinese rose dew,* cherry brandy or crème de menthe)	2 tablespoons sweet liqueur (Chinese rose dew,* cherry brandy or crème de menthe)

Stand the pears in a saucepan and just cover with water. Bring to the boil over a low heat and simmer for 30 minutes. Pour off half the water. Sprinkle the pears with the sugar and simmer for another 10 minutes. Remove the pears from the pan and chill in the refrigerator for 2 hours.

Pour off half the water remaining in the pan. Add the honey and liqueur to the pan and stir until well blended. Chill the sauce in the refrigerator for 2 hours.

Arrange the pears in individual dishes. Pour the honey sauce over and serve. SERVES 4.

Gingered Fruit; Mow Flower Twists; Jujube Cakes; Steamed Honeyed Pears

Glossary

Bamboo shoots Widely used in Chinese cooking. Canned bamboo shoots are most commonly used. They should be drained before use.

Bean curd Made of puréed and pressed soy beans, its texture is like soft cheese. Sold in cakes, 7.5 cm/3 inches square and 2.5 cm/1 inch thick. It will keep fresh for several days if stored in water in the refrigerator. Available from Oriental stores and some health food shops.

Bean curd cheese Made by fermenting small cubes of bean curd in wine and salt. Available in 2 varieties, red and white, both of which are available in jars and cans. Very salty and strong-tasting.

Bean sprouts These are the sprouts of small mung beans, which are available fresh and canned. They can be grown indoors at any time of the year and, in properly controlled conditions, will sprout in a very few days. Bean sprouts are at their best when cooked for only a very short time to retain their crispness.

Chinese rose dew Distilled from sorghum and other grains, it is blended with rose petals and aromatic herbs.

Chinese snow pickle Salted mustard greens. It is greenish in colour and has a salty, mildly sour flavour.

Chow Chow A preserve of ginger and orange peel and other fruits in syrup.

Five spice powder Made from a mixture of star anise, anise pepper (Szechuan peppercorns), cloves and cinnamon. Very pungent, it should be used sparingly. Normally used to season red-cooked (soy braised) or roasted meat and poultry.

Ginger, root Fresh root ginger, sometimes referred to as 'green ginger'. Peel before using, then slice, crush or chop finely. To keep fresh: peel, then wash and place in a jar, cover with pale dry sherry, seal and store in the refrigerator. Ground ginger is not an acceptable substitute, but dried root ginger may be used, in which case the quantity should be decreased as it is sharper in taste.

Glutinous (sweet) rice Also sometimes referred to as 'sticky rice'. Short-grain rice that becomes very sticky when cooked. Used in stuffings, cakes and puddings.

Glutinous (sweet) rice flour Made from ground glutinous (sweet) rice. There is no substitute. Obtainable from Chinese supermarkets.

Hoisin sauce Also known as Chinese barbecue sauce. Made from soy beans, flour, sugar, spices and red food colouring. Available in jars or cans from Chinese supermarkets, it will keep for several months in the refrigerator.

Monosodium Glutamate (MSG) A chemical compound sometimes known as 'taste essence'. It is used to bring out the natural flavours in food, and is entirely optional in all recipes where it is specified. It should be used sparingly: $\frac{1}{4}-\frac{1}{2}$ teaspoon is ample in any recipe. Obtainable from most oriental stores.

Mushrooms, dried Chinese dried mushrooms are sold in plastic bags in Oriental stores. They are very fragrant, and will keep almost indefinitely in an airtight jar. Soak in warm water for 30 minutes before using. Ordinary mushrooms do not make a good substitute.

Oyster sauce A thickish brown sauce with a rich flavour. Made from oysters and soy sauce. It keeps indefinitely in the refrigerator.

Rock sugar Known as rock candy in North America. It is crystallized sugar, amber in colour, which is used to give a glaze to certain dishes. 1 lump rock sugar is equivalent to 1 tablespoon granulated sugar.

Salted black beans Need to be soaked in cold water 5–10 minutes before use to remove excess salt. Used with fish or meat, often stir-fried.

Sesame paste Made from ground sesame seeds. It imparts a nutty flavour and combines well with soy sauce.

Sesame seed oil A strongly-flavoured seasoning oil made from roasted sesame seeds. Used for its fragrance and the flavour it imparts to other foods. Sold in bottles. Keeps indefinitely.

Shrimps, dried Available whole, pounded or powdered, from Oriental stores.

Soy bean paste Also known as brown-bean sauce. It is sold in cans and jars in Chinese food stores. It is often used instead of soy sauce when a thicker sauce is required in stir-fry cooking. Because of its saltiness, it acts as a preservative and is often cooked with meat to be served cold.

Soy sauce Is extensively used in Chinese cooking. As it is salty guard against using it excessively. It is best used with other ingredients, such as wine, sugar and stock. It adds savouriness to cooked food.

Star anise A fragrant-smelling spice and one of the ingredients of five spice powder.

Sweet bean paste/Sweet red bean paste See Sweet Soy Bean Paste.

Sweet soy bean paste Also called Red Bean Paste, is a thick paste (sauce) sold in cans. Use it as a dip, as a base for sweet sauces, or to accompany crispy dishes.

Transparent (cellophane) noodles Also called 'bean threads' and 'vermicelli'. Opaque, white threads which become transparent and expand upon soaking. In Chinese food stores they are sold in packets – in fluffy bundles which resemble candy floss (cotton candy). These noodles are never eaten on their own; they are usually added to soups or used in 'soup-type' dishes because they absorb quantities of stock which renders them highly savoury. The noodles should be soaked in hot water for 5 minutes before use.

Water chestnuts A walnut-sized bulb with brown skin; the inside flesh is white and crisp. Canned water chestnuts are ready-peeled and will keep for about 1 month in the refrigerator.

Wood (tree) ears Known as tree ear in North America, cloud ear in China. A dried tree fungus. Use only in small quantities. Soak in warm water for about 20 minutes before using, until glutinous and crinkly. The dried fungi will keep indefinitely. Available at Chinese supermarkets.

Yellow bean sauce Also known as brown or black bean sauce. Crushed yellow soy beans, mixed to a paste with flour, vinegar, spices and salt. Sold in jars and cans.

Index

Acknowledgments

Photography by Bryce Atwell 2–3, 4–5, 6–7; Robert Golden 10–11,
15, 16–17, 29, 32–33, 44–45, 46–47, 56–57, 78–79; Melvin Grey 9, 19,
21, 39, 40–41, 46–47, 50–51, 61, 66, 77, 81; Paul Kemp 20.

Special photography by Robert Golden 1, 12–13, 22–23, 25, 27, 30–31,
35, 36–37, 42–43, 48–49, 52–53, 54–55, 59, 62–63, 64–65, 66–67, 69,
70–71, 72–73, 74–75, 82–83, 85, 86–87, 88–89, 90–91, 93.
Photographic stylist Antonia Gaunt.
The publishers would like to thank the following for the loan of
accessories for photography: Paul Wu, 64 Long Acre, London WC2;
Neal Street East, 5 Neal Street, London WC2.